# DC COMICS
# SUPER HEROES

# CHARACTER ENCYCLOPEDIA
WRITTEN BY SIMON HUGO AND CAVAN SCOTT

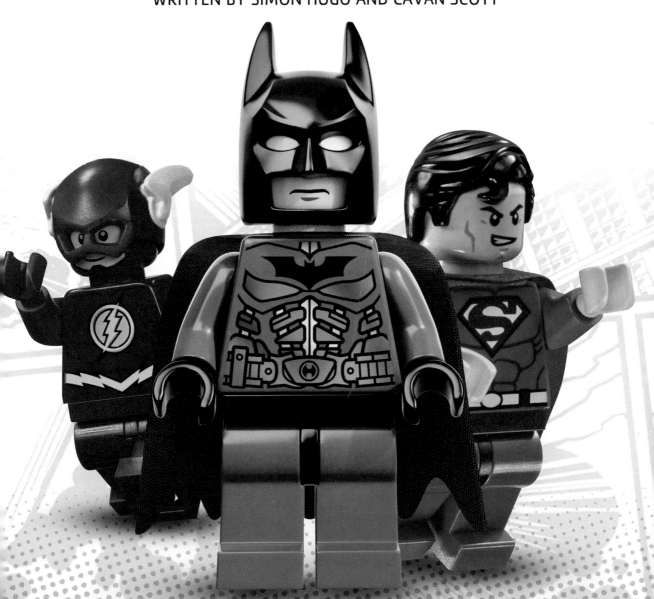

# CONTENTS

# ENTER
## THE WORLD OF LEGO®
## DC COMICS SUPER HEROES!

**Brave LEGO® DC Comics Super Heroes** take many forms—from the superpowered to the purely courageous with high-tech gear and gadgets. The villains they face are dangerously varied—and their minifigure counterparts are equally so!

### HOW TO USE THIS BOOK

This book is a comprehensive guide to ten years of LEGO DC Comics Super Heroes minifigures, vehicles, and explosive sets! Minifigures and vehicles are ordered chronologically according to when they were released, from 2006–2016.

# BRUCE WAYNE
## TO THE MANOR BORN

## VITAL STATS
...............................

**LIKES:** Bats
**DISLIKES:** Bats (Bruce is a complex guy!)
**FRIENDS:** Alfred
**FOES:** Anyone who might discover his secret identity
**SKILLS:** Brilliant businessman
**GEAR:** Secret hideout

**SET NAMES:** The Batcave: The Penguin and Mr. Freeze's Invasion
**SET NUMBERS:** 7783
**YEARS:** 2006

### DID YOU KNOW?
Wayne Enterprises includes Wayne Technologies, Wayne Medical, Wayne Foods, Wayne Weapons, Wayne Airlines, Wayne Energy, Wayne Entertainment, and more!

Classic LEGO® hair, around since 1979!

Same smirk as Colonel Hardy (p.91)

Sharp suit also used in LEGO® Indiana Jones™ theme

### BECOMING BATMAN
A bridge in Bruce's Batcave leads to a gym and a chamber where Bruce can change into his Batsuit. But beware! It also has a trapdoor to a cage below.

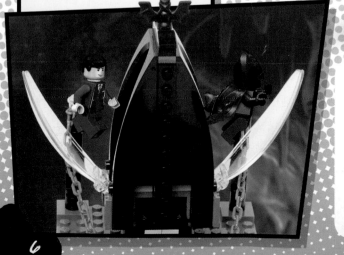

**Bruce is the billionaire** boss of Wayne Enterprises. He raises money for charity through the Wayne Foundation, throws lavish parties, and often features in Gotham City's gossip columns. (He's also secretly Batman—but don't tell anybody!)

# BATMAN
## THE MAN IN BLACK

BATMAN

### VITAL STATS

**LIKES:** Gotham City
**DISLIKES:** Crime
**FRIENDS:** Commissioner Gordon
**FOES:** The Joker
**SKILLS:** Scaring bad guys
**GEAR:** Bulletproof armor, Utility Belt

**SET NAMES:** The Batmobile: Two-Face's Escape, The Batcave: The Penguin and Mr. Freeze's Invasion, Arkham Asylum
**SET NUMBERS:** 7781, 7783, 7785
**YEARS:** 2006

### DID YOU KNOW?

An exclusive San Diego Comic-Con giveaway in 2005 included this version of Batman along with the Joker (see p.24).

Pointy bat ears for a scary silhouette!

Armor molded around muscles

Utility Belt can carry grapple gun and smoke bombs

### BAT PACK

Batman can't fly like Superman, but when the Riddler, Scarecrow, and Poison Ivy break out of Arkham Asylum (set 7785), he tracks them down using this giant bat-shaped jetpack.

**Batman is the protector** of Gotham City. When the Bat-Signal shines in the sky, he answers the call to action—sweeping in from the shadows or blasting onto the scene in his Batmobile.

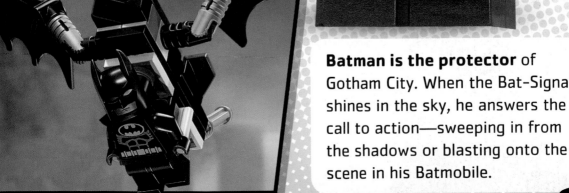

7

# BATMAN
## THE CAPED CRUSADER

## VITAL STATS
........................

**LIKES:** Big pockets for tools
**DISLIKES:** Criminals running amok in Gotham City
**FRIENDS:** Robin
**FOES:** The Riddler, Bane, Scarecrow
**SKILLS:** Criminology
**GEAR:** Bat-cuffs

**SET NAMES:** The Batcopter: The Chase for Scarecrow, The Bat-Tank: The Riddler and Bane's Hideout
**SET NUMBERS:** 7786, 7787
**YEARS:** 2007

### DID YOU KNOW?
There have been at least 30 different bat-symbols since Batman's comic-book debut in 1940.

Blue cowl looks good in the moonlight!

Simple bat-symbol

Chunky Utility Belt

**2007**

Lead-lined cowl

Arched bat-symbol

Five-pointed cape echoes bat-symbol

## VITAL STATS
........................

**LIKES:** Not being seen
**DISLIKES:** Smiling for photos
**FRIENDS:** Alfred
**FOES:** The Joker, Catwoman, Killer Croc
**SKILLS:** Nighttime camouflage
**GEAR:** Batwing launcher

**SET NAMES:** The Batman Dragster: Catwoman Pursuit, The Batboat: Hunt for Killer Croc, The Batwing: The Joker's Aerial Assault
**SET NUMBERS:** 7779, 7780, 7782
**YEARS:** 2006

**2006**

**LIKES:** Dark nights
**DISLIKES:** Bright colors
**FRIENDS:** Commissioner Gordon
**FOES:** The Joker, Harley Quinn, Mr. Freeze
**SKILLS:** Extreme physical endurance
**GEAR:** Batarangs

**SET NAMES:** Batman's Buggy: The Escape of Mr. Freeze, The Batcycle: Harley Quinn's Hammer Truck, The Tumbler: Joker's Ice Cream Surprise
**SET NUMBERS:** 7884, 7886, 7888
**YEARS:** 2008

Listening device in right ear of cowl

Flexible kevlar armor

**2008**

Utility Belt includes Tumbler remote control

### COMIC CHARACTER

At the San Diego Comic-Con in 2011 this exclusive Batman minifigure was released to mark the relaunch of the LEGO DC Comics Super Heroes range. His armor is darker and tougher.

### DID YOU KNOW?

All Batman minifigures released before 2011 have the same face printing, with serious eyes, a stern mouth, and a white sweatband.

**The Caped Crusader** dresses to impress, updating his outfits as crime fighting fashion dictates. Blue, black, and gray are his go-to colors, with a belt to add a bit of bling. But while the details may change, the iconic cape and cowl mean he's always unmistakably Batman!

# BATMOBILE
## BACK IN TOWN

## VITAL STATS
............................

**OWNER:** Batman
**USED FOR:** Catching crooks
**GEAR:** Mega-missile

**SET NAME:** The Batmobile:
Two-Face's Escape
**SET NUMBER:** 7781
**YEAR:** 2006

Power flows to
all four wheels
via chunky pipes

Flexible fins
shaped like
bats' wings

Lever
launches
missile

Rubber-
nosed missile

### BATMAN'S BUGGY
The Caped Crusader pursues
another crook in Batman's Buggy:
The Escape of Mr. Freeze (set
7884). His Buggy is smaller than
the Batmobile, but still stops
traffic with its built-in gadgets.

Headlights are
stickers

**This version** of the Batmobile
packs a real punch, with a huge
missile loaded between the front
wheels. When Batman uses this
surprise weapon against Two-
Face, it blasts the villain right off
the roof of his getaway truck!

Tail fin reduces drag

### DID YOU KNOW?
The fastest racing dragsters can reach speeds over 300 miles per hour!

## VITAL STATS
..................

**OWNER** Batman
**USED FOR:** High-speed chases
**GEAR:** Missiles, laser cannon

**SET NAME:** The Batman Dragster: Catwoman Pursuit
**SET NUMBER:** 7779
**YEAR:** 2006

Rotating laser cannon

### CANNON-FACING
A hidden front wheel steers the dragster left and right. The laser cannon turns with the wheel, so that it is always pointing to wherever the dragster is going.

Missile launcher

Cooling vent

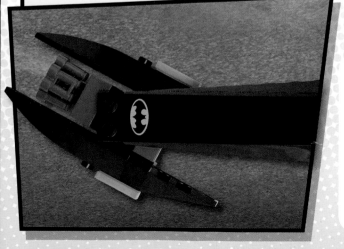

**Batman built this dragster** for speed. Where wider vehicles are slowed by the wind, this dart-like design can slice through Gotham City's streets like a scythe. Its shape and speed also make it a hard target to hit in a battle.

## BATMAN'S BUTLER

Bald head
accompanies
wise expression

Classic LEGO goblet
for taking refreshment
to Batman

Alfred's suit rivals
those of the
Penguin's!

### SOME ICE, SIR?
Alfred rarely battles bad guys,
but when the Batcave is
attacked, he doesn't lose his
cool. In fact, he seems positively
chilled when Mr. Freeze traps
him in a block of ice!

**Alfred Pennyworth** is one of the
few people trusted with Batman's
biggest secret: his other identity
as Bruce Wayne! He provides loyal
service at Wayne Manor—and
beneath it in the Batcave.

# ROBIN
## *TRUSTED SIDEKICK*

## VITAL STATS

**LIKES:** Working things out
**DISLIKES:** Unsolved puzzles
**FRIENDS:** Batman, Alfred, Nightwing
**FOES:** The Penguin, Mr. Freeze
**SKILLS:** Deduction, swimming
**GEAR:** Scuba jet

**SET NAMES:** Robin's Scuba Jet: Attack of The Penguin
**SET NUMBERS:** 7885
**YEARS:** 2008

Both 2006 and 2008 Robin minifigures variants wear the same outfit with a bright yellow cape.

Flat hairpiece has also appeared in LEGO® Pharaoh's Quest and LEGO® City sets.

"R" on chest is a stylized throwing star

### BIRD ON THE WATER
The Boy Wonder made a splash with a different hairstyle when he sped into battle on his jet ski in The Batcave: The Penguin and Mr. Freeze's Invasion (set 7783) in 2006.

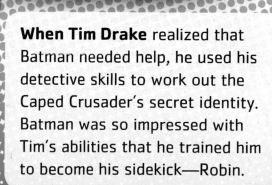

**When Tim Drake** realized that Batman needed help, he used his detective skills to work out the Caped Crusader's secret identity. Batman was so impressed with Tim's abilities that he trained him to become his sidekick—Robin.

**THE BATCAVE**
The first of three LEGO Batcaves, this design, from set 7783, features a Batcomputer displaying Batman's Rogues Gallery and a Mr. Freeze intent on trapping Alfred the butler!

THOOM!

NAME: Harvey Dent
ALIAS: Two-Face
BASE: Unknown

THE PENGUIN? MORE LIKE THE CHICKEN! STOP RUNNING AWAY!

## VITAL STATS

**OWNED BY:** Robin
**USED FOR:** Deep-water diving
**GEAR:** Breathable atmosphere, rocket launchers

**SET NAMES:** Robin's Scuba Jet: Attack of The Penguin
**SET NUMBERS:** 7885
**YEARS:** 2008

Color scheme with "R" symbols matches Robin's costume.

## BIRD STRIKE

Robin knows when he's close to the Penguin's Submarine—that's when the Penguin sends his robot helpers to attack. These robo-penguins work just as well under water as on land!

Blaster weapons designed to work underwater.

Large, clear canopy gives Robin a wide sea-view.

These green engines do not appear in any other LEGO set.

**Robin can** breathe easy as he dives deep in pursuit of the Penguin. His Scuba Jet has its own air supply so he can stay underwater for extended periods—although its twin turbine engines should bring any chase to a speedy end.

# NIGHTWING
## SOLO FLYER

### VITAL STATS
........................

**LIKES:** Acrobatics
**DISLIKES:** Being told what
to do
**FRIENDS:** Batman
**FOES:** Poison Ivy
**SKILLS:** Martial arts
**GEAR:** Escrima sticks

**SET NAMES:** Arkham Asylum
**SET NUMBERS:** 7785
**YEARS:** 2006

Rubber hairpiece
created for
LEGO® EXO-
FORCE™ theme in
2006.

Mask shaped
like wings
spread in flight

Blue and black
costume also echoes
the wingspan of a
bird or a dragon.

### NIGHT RIDER

Nightwing rides this streamlined cycle to help Batman foil an escape from Arkham Asylum (set 7785). It has space for his two martial arts fighting sticks, also known as escrima, at the back.

**Dick Grayson** was the first Robin, fighting crime alongside Batman. As he grew older, he wanted to go his own way. He chose Nightwing as his new identity after Superman told him about a legendary Kryptonian character with the same name.

# CATWOMAN

## GOTHAM CITY'S NUMBER ONE CAT BURGLAR

### VITAL STATS

**LIKES:** Diamonds
**DISLIKES:** Getting caught
**FRIENDS:** Batman
**FOES:** Batman
**SKILLS:** Quick getaways
**GEAR:** Whip

**SET NAMES:** Catwoman
Catcycle City Chase
**SET NUMBERS:** 6858
**YEARS:** 2012

### DID YOU KNOW?
Catwoman appears in all three of the LEGO® Batman video games, along with her cat, Isis.

Mask doubles as a Catcycle helmet

White goggles keep Catwoman's eyes hidden

Catwoman's 2012 costume comes complete with a chunkier zip and belt.

### LITTLE BLACK CATSUIT

Catwoman's 2006 minifigure wears a stealthy black catsuit with a matching black mask and simpler torso detailing. Armed with her trusty whip, this cat burglar is ready to tangle with Batman in The Batman Dragster: Catwoman Pursuit (set 7779).

**Glamorous Selina Kyle** has a weakness for glittering diamonds. No gem is safe while Catwoman is on the prowl. A talented gymnast, Selina often has to make acrobatic escapes from Batman.

# CATCYCLE
## MEEEEEOWWWWW!

**VITAL STATS**
• • • • • • • • • • • • • • • • • • • • • •

**OWNER:** Catwoman
**USED FOR:** Cat burglary
**GEAR:** Whip

**SET NAME:** Catwoman
Catcycle City Chase
**SET NUMBER:** 6858
**YEAR:** 2012

Stolen diamond

In-built grip for a whip

Kickstand in raised position

## EYES ON THE ROAD
The Catcycle in The Batman Dragster: Catwoman Pursuit (set 7779) has cat's eyes and ears at the front, and an exhaust flame trailing like a cat's tail.

**Speeding like a cheetah**, Selina Kyle's catlike bike can whisk her from crime scene to crime scene with barely a pause. Her two wheels purr along nicely—whether she's driving to commit the crimes or solve them.

# KILLER CROC
## COLD-BLOODED CROOK

Exclusive scaly
face printing

Narrowed red
eyes

Scales continue on
unique torso printing.

## SCALE MODEL

Killer Croc does his best to
outpace the Batboat in this
small speedboat. Part of the
character's only LEGO set
appearance to date, it features
exclusive crocodile-face printing
and swamp-green missiles.

**With a grin** to rival the Joker's,
this reptilian rascal could snap at
any moment! He may not have
much in the way of brains, but his
tough, scaly skin and super-
strength make him the mean, green
king of Gotham City's swamps.

# THE BATBOAT
## BAT ON THE WATER

Bat-shaped wings leave no doubt who owns this craft!

Twin propellers are linked and turn together.

Space to store jet ski behind cockpit

### CRAFTY GETAWAY

A one-person jet ski fits into the back of the Batboat. Small enough to speed along narrow rivers or even sewers, it's the perfect craft to pursue Killer Croc's speedboat.

**This heavily armed hovercraft** is ideal for chasing Killer Croc. Like all hovercraft, it can skim over water or land on a cushion of air, and is powered by large propellers. Unlike other hovercraft, it also has a pair of cool bat-shaped wings!

# TWO-FACE
## DON'T GET ON HIS BAD SIDE!

TWO FACE

## VITAL STATS

**LIKES:** Playing heads or tails
**DISLIKES:** Matching outfits
**FRIENDS:** His other half
**FOES:** Batman
**SKILLS:** Seeing things from both sides
**GEAR:** Machine gun, lucky coin

**SET NAMES:** The Batmobile: Two-Face's Escape
**SET NUMBERS:** 7781
**YEARS:** 2006

Unruly hair on left-hand side of head.

Purple facial scarring only covers left-hand side of face.

White suit on dark-haired side... and dark suit on white-haired side!

## SPLITTING HAIRS

Two-Face was the first LEGO minifigure to have multicolored hair—made from white plastic with black printing. Poison Ivy and Wonder Woman also have printing on their hair pieces.

**Lots of people** in Gotham City lead double lives, but Two-Face takes it to extremes! One of the city's biggest crime bosses, he is in two minds about everything and makes decisions by flipping his lucky coin—unlucky for some!

# THUG'S HENCHY
## BANDED BANDIT

## VITAL STATS
..........................

**LIKES:** Black and white
**DISLIKES:** Sorting laundry
**FRIENDS:** Two-Face's
right side
**FOES:** Two-Face's wrong
side... or is it the other
way around?
**SKILLS:** Bank robbery
**GEAR:** Handgun

**SET NAMES:** The Batmobile:
Two-Face's Escape
**SET NUMBERS:** 7781
**YEARS:** 2006

Black and white
jersey echoes
Two-Face's suit

Black
handgun

## HEELS ON WHEELS
The bank truck hijacked by
Two-Face and his Henchman
boasts an armored windshield, a
booby-trapped roof, and hidden
weapons that fold out from the
sides of the vehicle.

**What's black and white** and green
all over? A stolen Gotham City Bank
truck filled with banknotes and
Two-Face's goon! This Henchman
is always happy to help out with
a bank heist—though you wouldn't
know it from the look on his face!

23

# THE JOKER
## THE CLOWN PRINCE OF CRIME

Unique green hair piece with pointed edges

Laughter lines round eyes and mouth from too much grinning

Don't sniff the flower—it spits acid!

### FUN IN THE GUN

The Joker's armory of outlandish weapons ranges from the silly to the scary. One of his favorites is a gun that fires a flag with the word "BANG!" written on it.

BANG!

**This clownish character** is no fool: he's the prince of crime in Gotham City! His grin hides a deep hatred of Batman and Robin, and his jokes always have a sting in the tail. He is out to cause chaos at every comic turn!

# THE JOKER'S HENCHMAN

## WILL WORK FOR SNACKS

### VITAL STATS
..........................

**LIKES:** Popsicles
**DISLIKES:** Brain freeze
**FRIENDS:** The Joker,
Mr. Freeze
**FOES:** Batman and Robin
**SKILLS:** Flying the Joker's
helicopter
**GEAR:** Nice hat

**SET NAMES:** The Batwing:
The Joker's Aerial Assault,
The Tumbler: Joker's Ice
Cream Surprise
**SET NUMBERS:** 7782, 7888
**YEARS:** 2006, 2008

Classic henchman hat

Purple top matches
the Joker's jacket

Popsicle from the
Joker's Ice-Cream Van

## IT'S THAT MAN AGAIN

A familiar-looking Henchman
also assists Mr. Freeze in The
Batcave: The Penguin and Mr.
Freeze's Invasion (set 7783).
He wears a blue top and black
gloves along with his usual hat.

**The Joker's Henchman** looks
remarkably like Two-Face's
Henchman (p.23). Perhaps he is the
same hired hand, prepared to do
the dirty work for whoever keeps
him stocked up with sunglasses
and knitted hats—or popsicles!

# THE HELI-COPTER
## SKY-HIGH SURPRISE

The Joker's Henchman is at the controls!

### VITAL STATS
....................

**OWNED BY:** The Joker
**USED FOR:** Dropping laughing gas on Gotham
**GEAR:** Missiles, gas bombs

**SET NAMES:** The Batwing: The Joker's Aerial Assault
**SET NUMBERS:** 7782
**YEARS:** 2006

Copter sides fold down to reveal missiles

### BOMBS AWAY
Pulling the rod at the back of the Copter releases grinning green gas bombs from a hidden compartment. The Joker also likes to throw these while hanging from the rope ladder!

Detachable rope ladder held in place with LEGO® Technic pin

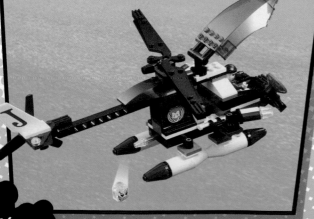

**This helicopter** looks harmless— until its sides fold down to reveal hidden weapons! Part of the Joker's plan to cover Gotham City with toxic laughing gas, it can also use its side-mounted satellite dish to deflect missiles from Batman's Batwing.

# THE CHILLING JOKE

## VITAL STATS

**OWNED BY:** The Joker
**USED FOR:** Selling Joker-gas ice creams
**GEAR:** Missile launcher

**SET NAMES:** The Tumbler: Joker's Ice Cream Surprise
**SET NUMBERS:** 7888
**YEARS:** 2008

Missile launcher disguised within giant multi-colored ice-cream scoops

Logo promises a surprise—but not a nice one!

Spring-loaded missile

## NOT-SO-NICE CREAM

Three very unpleasant sounding flavors of ice cream are listed on the back of the Joker's truck: Soda Smile Pop Sickle, Ol' Fashioned Venom Flavor, and Rigor Mortis Soft Ice!

Venom for making toxic ice creams goes inside slots labelled "venom."

License plate reads "I Scream."

**The colorful cone** on top of this truck isn't just for show—it's also a lever that fires a giant missile out through the back doors! The Joker will need this secret weapon when Batman hears about his tasteless plan to sell toxic gas ice creams.

# BATWING
## A SYMBOL OF HOPE

### VITAL STATS
..........................

**OWNER:** Batman
**USED FOR:** Aerial battles
**GEAR:** Missile launcher, rockets

**SET NAME:** The Batwing: The Joker's Aerial Assault
**SET NUMBER:** 7782
**YEAR:** 2006

Missile launcher folds away into tail

Missile in flight

Back wings lift to reveal rockets

### LANDING GEAR

The Batwing has its own landing bay in the Batcave, with a folding ladder that leads to the cockpit. It is always ready for vertical take-off, straight up into the sky.

Forward prongs can snare enemies in mid-air

**If Gotham City** comes under attack from the air, Batman takes to the skies in this special fighter jet. It is shaped like the bat-symbol, so that the citizens below can look up and see that the Caped Crusader is on the case.

# BATCOPTER
## FLYING WITHOUT WINGS

### VITAL STATS
........................

**OWNER:** Batman
**USED FOR:** Patrolling the skies
**GEAR:** Lasers, rockets, missile

**SET NAME:** The Batcopter: The Chase for Scarecrow
**SET NUMBER:** 7786
**YEAR:** 2007

Rotor blades fold up when not in use

Targeting display

Air-to-air missile

Jet fuel goes in here

Twin laser cannons

## CROW VS. BAT
When Batman battles the Scarecrow, he needs a biplane-busting missile to stop the raggedy wrongdoer from dropping fear-gas bombs on the people below!

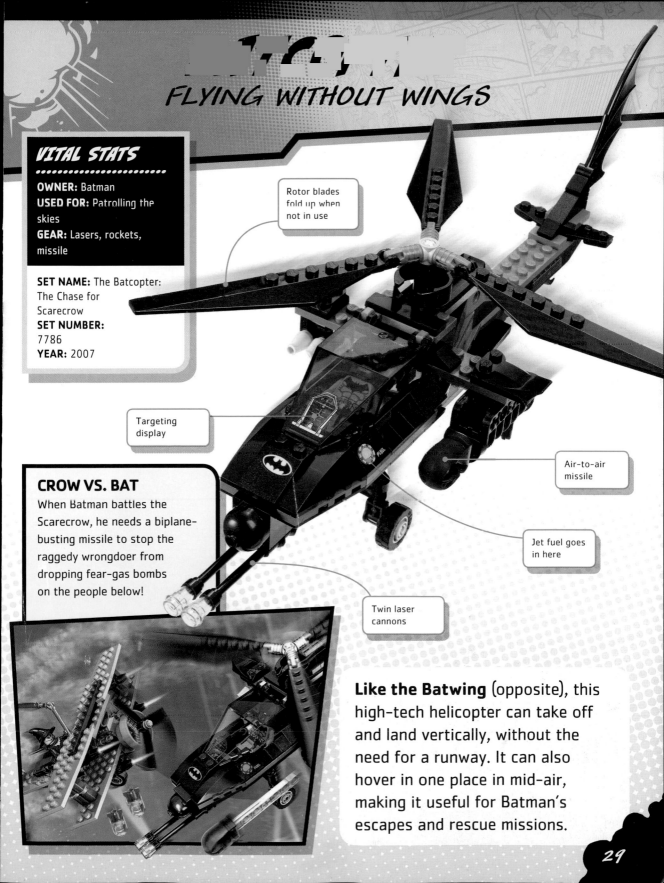

**Like the Batwing** (opposite), this high-tech helicopter can take off and land vertically, without the need for a runway. It can also hover in one place in mid-air, making it useful for Batman's escapes and rescue missions.

29

# THE PENGUIN
## FREE AS A BIRD

### DID YOU KNOW?
The original 2006
Penguin minifigure
didn't have an eye
showing through
his monocle.

Monocle

Umbrella doubles
as a weapon

Purple
mini-legs

### DRESSED TO IMPRESS
Batman's oldest foe, the Penguin
fancies himself as an upstanding
Gotham City citizen. Always
impeccably dressed, the original
2006 Penguin minifigure wore
an elegant tuxedo with an
orange waistcoat in sets 7783
and 7885.

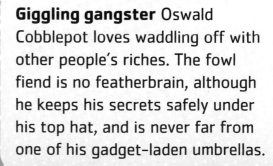

**Giggling gangster** Oswald
Cobblepot loves waddling off with
other people's riches. The fowl
fiend is no featherbrain, although
he keeps his secrets safely under
his top hat, and is never far from
one of his gadget-laden umbrellas.

# THE PENGUIN SUBMARINE

## SWIMMING WITH THE FISHES

### VITAL STATS
**OWNER:** The Penguin
**USED FOR:** Jewel theft
**GEAR:** Missiles fore and aft

**SET NAME:** Robin's Scuba Jet: Attack of The Penguin
**SET NUMBER:** 7885
**YEAR:** 2008

Torpedo launcher

Periscope for seeing what's going on above water

Tower section lifts off

Intimidating Penguin face on prow

Lever fires a missile from the stern

The Penguin's tally of Bat battles!

## GOING UNDERGROUND

With Mr. Freeze on board, the Penguin sets course for Batman's secret base in The Batcave: The Penguin and Mr. Freeze's Invasion (set 7783). This earlier sub is labelled U98 on the side.

**Numbered U99** (the "U" stands for "undersea"), this sub swims as well as a real seabird! On the hull, the Penguin has marked the fact that he has fought four battles with Batman, and is now hoping to get away with a stolen crystal!

# MR. FREEZE
## COLD-HEARTED SCIENTIST

Goggles worn over eyes that are capable of producing icy blasts

Helmet keeps this criminal cool

Freeze ray puts enemies on ice

Backpack pumps coolant round suit

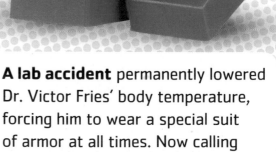

## STONE COLD STEAL

Mr. Freeze wields a different ray gun as he makes his getaway from a diamond robbery. Driving a sub-zero speedster, he hopes to freeze Batman's pursuing Buggy in its tracks!

**A lab accident** permanently lowered Dr. Victor Fries' body temperature, forcing him to wear a special suit of armor at all times. Now calling himself Mr. Freeze, he turned to crime to fund his scientific research.

# POISON IVY
## NAUGHTY BY NATURE

### VITAL STATS
......................

**LIKES:** Plants and flowers
**DISLIKES:** Pesticides
**FRIENDS:** Bane
**FOES:** Batman and Robin
**SKILLS:** Biology, plant control
**GEAR:** Twisted vines

**SET NAMES:** The Batcave, Batman: Arkham Asylum Breakout, Jokerland
**SET NUMBERS:** 6860, 10937, 76035
**YEARS:** 2012, 2013, 2015

Leaves curl through Ivy's flaming red hair.

A kiss from these sly lips will soon make you snooze.

## THE ECO-WARRIOR

The 2006 Poison Ivy minifigure had exclusive dark red hair, green lips, and black eyes with light green eye shadow. Although a brilliant botanist, she would still love to escape her greenhouse-styled prison in Arkham Asylum (set 7785).

Poison Ivy's leafy costume is also printed on the back.

**As twisted as her** beloved vines, Poison Ivy just wants to save the environment—from the human race. Able to control plants by the power of her mind, Ivy is immune to all poisons. Just don't let her pucker up for a kiss!

# THE SCARECROW
## MASTER OF FEAR

### VITAL STATS

**LIKES:** Striking fear into the hearts of everyone
**DISLIKES:** Bullies
**FRIENDS:** The Arkham Asylum inmates
**FOES:** Batman and Robin
**SKILLS:** Escape bids
**GEAR:** Scarecrow hat

**SET NAME:** Batman: Arkham Asylum Breakout
**SET NUMBER:** 10937
**YEAR:** 2013

Wide-brimmed scarecrow hat

Scary cloth face

Rope fashion accessories

His tattered clothing is also printed on the back of the minifigure.

### LIVING NIGHTMARE

Luckily, Scarecrow doesn't have Nyctophobia, fear of the dark, or Cleithrophobia, fear of being locked up, as he spends lots of time in jail. Not that it would matter, as his earlier 2006 minifigure, in set 7786, had a glow-in-the-dark head!

**Shunned by his** friends and family, phobia expert Dr. Jonathan Crane decided to terrify everyone in Gotham City. As the Scarecrow, he uses his homemade fear gas to bring his victims' worst nightmares to life.

# SCARECROW'S STRIKE

## AS THE CROW FLIES

### VITAL STATS

**OWNER:** Scarecrow
**USED FOR:** Fear gas attacks
**GEAR:** Fear gas bombs,
machine guns

**SET NAME:** The Batcopter:
The Chase for Scarecrow
**SET NUMBER:** 7786
**YEAR:** 2007

Scarecrow holds
onto his scythe
while flying

Biplanes take
their name from
having two sets
of wings.

Scary scarecrow
face on tail fin

### GREEN FEAR GAS BOMBS

As well as having
two tanks of fear
gas ready to spray, Scarecrow's
Biplane is also equipped with
fear gas bombs. Colored the
same ghastly green, they have
horrible grinning pumpkin
heads inside!

Spinning
propeller

One of four
machine guns

**Scarecrow scythes** through the sky
in his biplane. It might look old-
fashioned, but its four machine guns
are very high-tech: perfectly placed
to fire between moving rotor blades.
Plus it carries weapons that are the
cutting-edge of criminal chemistry!

35

# THE RIDDLER
## GOTHAM CITY'S CLUED-UP CRIMINAL

### VITAL STATS

**LIKES:** Dangling sidekicks from cranes
**DISLIKES:** Straight talking
**FRIENDS:** The Joker, Harley Quinn
**FOES:** Batman and Robin
**SKILLS:** Creating riddles
**GEAR:** Question-mark cane

**SET NAMES:** The Dynamic Duo Funhouse Escape
**SET NUMBERS:** 6857
**YEARS:** 2012

**DID YOU KNOW?**
The Dynamic Duo Funhouse Escape set includes a mini-Riddler mannequin in the ticket office.

The 2012 Riddler minifigure now wears a bowler hat in place of black hair.

Defined muscles show through green suit.

There's no question about the Ridder's favorite punctuation mark!

### CARRIED AWAY
In 2006, the Riddler was carted off to Arkham Asylum (set 7785) sporting a shock of black hair and a slightly simpler green outfit. This variant also cropped up in The Bat-Tank: The Riddler and Bane's Hideout (set 7787).

**One of Gotham City's** most confusing villains, Edward Nygma likes to leave a trail of cryptic clues to help Batman foil his crimes. No one knows why. It's a complete mystery, and the most puzzling of all of the Riddler's riddles.

# BAT-TANK
## CAN'T BE STOPPED IN ITS TRACKS!

### VITAL STATS

**OWNER:** Batman
**USED FOR:** Going where other land vehicles can't go
**GEAR:** Missiles, rockets

**SET NAMES:** The Bat-Tank: The Riddler and Bane's Hideout
**SET NUMBERS:** 7787
**YEARS:** 2007

Batman is well protected lying down inside the Bat-Tank

### DID YOU KNOW?
Batman has more than 10 different Batmobiles, but only one Bat-Tank!

Triple missile launcher comes with yellow side missiles and a rubber-nosed rocket.

### ENTER THROUGH GATE
The bunker-busting Bat-Tank has no problem breaking in to Bane's fortified hideout, easily knocking down the chained-up gates that come with this set.

Caterpillar tracks turn on inner wheels

**What's a Super Hero** to do when he already owns cars, motorcycles, boats, planes, and helicopters? Get a tank, of course! Batman's Bat-Tank has huge tracks for crawling over tough terrain and a weapons turret with two types of missile.

# HARLEY QUINN
## DIAMOND DEVIANT

A revolving head
reveals a
mischievous grin.

Harley Quinn was the
first LEGO minifigure
to wear a jester's hat.

## ARMED TO THE TEETH

The 2008 Harley Quinn from set
7886 had a wide, manic grin,
but had not yet learnt good
dental care—her teeth were
stained a horrible yellow color!
Mocking her looks, however,
is not advised, as she's equipped
with not one, but two, weapons!

The red and black
card game color
scheme continues
with diamond motifs.

**Harleen Quinzel** was the Joker's
doctor at Arkham Asylum, but
instead of curing her criminal
patient, she joined him on a crazy
crime spree as Harley Quinn. Now,
she has fun causing chaos in Gotham
City with her beloved puddin' Mr J!

# HARLEY'S HAMMER TRUCK

## MANIC MOTOR

Harley's minifigure holds yet another hammer.

"WHACK-A-BAT" scrawled on hammer

## HAMMER TIME

Batman rides a winged Batcycle in pursuit of Harley's Hammer Truck. Both his armor and the motorcycle have the same flat-topped bat-symbol up front.

Monster-truck wheels

**Look out:** Harley Quinn is hitting the streets—literally! Her mashing machine has a huge mechanical hammer to whack anything in its path. Batman had better move fast to stop her giving his Batcycle a flat tire—and a flat everything else!

# BANE
## BRAWN AND BRAINS COMBINED

Head encased in a mask so Bane can constantly breathe in Venom.

Artificially developed muscles

No gloves—Bane likes to break things with his bare hands

## THREE-WHEELING

Similar in dress apart from his blue trousers and slightly different head mask, the 2007 Bane still looks tough and brutish. He patrols his hideout in set 7787 on a three-wheeled dirt bike equipped with a missile launcher and a sidecar with a laser weapon.

**Don't be fooled by** all those muscles, super-villain Bane is no meathead. Able to speak dozens of different languages, this menacing mastermind uses a serum known as Venom to give himself super-strength and agility.

## READY TO RUMBLE

### VITAL STATS
....................

**OWNER:** Batman
**USED FOR:** Patrolling the mean streets of Gotham City
**GEAR:** Missiles, cannon

**SET NAME:** The Tumbler: Joker's Ice Cream Surprise
**SET NUMBER:** 7888
**YEAR:** 2008

Rear missiles hide beneath the Tumbler's sharp angles

### DID YOU KNOW?
The Tumbler was originally designed to leap across rivers and deploy bridges linking one side to the other.

Raised fins assist braking

Smaller front wheels for tight turns

### SECRET WEAPON
The back of the Tumbler has a hidden launcher that flips up to fire a large rubber-tipped missile. The missile can be locked in place with a LEGO® Technic pin.

Twin machine guns lie between the front wheels

**This angular assault vehicle** is heavily armed with two different types of missile. The cockpit has room for Batman and a passenger (or a handcuffed prisoner!), and four extra-large back wheels power the vehicle into battle.

# BATMAN
## CLASSIC-STYLE CAPED CRUSADER

### VITAL STATS

**LIKES:** Rescue missions
**DISLIKES:** Terrible traps
**FRIENDS:** Robin
**FOES:** The Joker, the Riddler,
Harley Quinn
**SKILLS:** Motorcycle stunts
**GEAR:** Batarangs, Batmobile

**SET NAMES:** The Dynamic
Duo Funhouse Escape,
The Batcave
**SET NUMBERS:** 6857, 6860
**YEARS:** 2012

Batman's eyes cannot be seen through his suit's cowl.

Fabric cloak for dramatic poses.

Batman's trusty Batarang has appeared in more than 20 LEGO sets.

Classic bat-symbol on a bright yellow disk.

### SPREADING HIS WINGS

To stop Catwoman from making a purr-fect getaway, Batman swaps his cape for glider wings and a jetpack to take to the air and chase after her in Catwoman Catcycle City Chase (set 6858).

Gadgets can be attached to Utility Belt.

**Heroic Batman dons** this classic comic book color scheme to free Robin from a fiendish funfair. His blue and gray suit is more than enough to strike terror into Gotham's super-villain community.

# THE JOKER
## STILL THINKS HE'S FUNNY

Yellow teeth revealed in wide grin on one side of head.

New waistcoat design features a lurid lime-green pattern.

### BEHIND THE SMILE
The Joker's manic laughter hides a keen intelligence. His fiendish plots are full of surprises, which is why a spin of this minifigure's head reveals a sneaky smirk.

Remote control for Joker's latest barmy bat-trap!

**Still mad, bad, and dangerous** to know, the Joker is up to his same, old tricks. With a yellow grin stretched across the chalk-white face of this minifigure variant, Batman's greatest enemy is about to launch his own brand of toxic laughing gas.

# BRUCE WAYNE

## CRIME-FIGHTING BILLIONAIRE

### VITAL STATS
..........................

**LIKES:** The Batcave
**DISLIKES:** Drill tanks
**FRIENDS:** Robin
**FOES:** Poison Ivy, Bane
**SKILLS:** A quick Bat-change
**GEAR:** Bat-phone

**SET NAME:** The Batcave
**SET NUMBER:** 6860
**YEAR:** 2012

**DID YOU KNOW?**
Bruce's stern expression is similar to the face you'll find under the Batman minifigure's cowl.

Slicked-back black hair

Chiseled cheekbones and a serious expression

A stylish sand-blue suit

### THE CALL TO ACTION
Bruce knows about trouble as soon as the phone rings. Luckily, the elevator is ready to transform him into Batman and drop him into the fight!

BAT-GEAR

**Billionaire Bruce Wayne** puts his vast riches to good use fighting crime as Batman, and yet his worse nightmares come true when Bane drills into the top-secret Batcave. Bruce doesn't want anyone to discover his secret identity.

# ROBIN
## OLDER BOY WONDER

## VITAL STATS

**LIKES:** Using his brains
**DISLIKES:** Being treated like a kid
**FRIENDS:** Batman
**FOES:** The Joker
**SKILLS:** Detecting
**GEAR:** Grappling hook

**SET NAMES:** The Dynamic Duo Funhouse Escape, The Batcave, Robin and the Redbird Cycle
**SET NUMBERS:** 6857, 6860, 30166
**YEARS:** 2012, 2012, 2013

Robin's head swivels to reveal a shocked expression for when facing the scariest of villains.

Fabric cape similar to Batman's

### BOY GENIUS AT WORK
Tim Drake is known as the Boy Wonder for a reason! He is a first-class scientist, engineer, and he can use the Batcomputer as well as Batman himself—maybe even better!

Utility Belt pouches hold everything a top sidekick needs!

**Stepping out on his own,** but still fighting crime as Robin, Tim Drake dons a more serious, all-red costume. The single color makes it look like Tim no longer has time for fun, and certainly this variant does not feature a smiling expression.

45

# BATCYCLE
## RIDING TO THE RESCUE

## VITAL STATS
..........................
**OWNER:** Batman
**USED FOR:** Rapid rescues
**GEAR:** Rocket boosters

**SET NAMES:** The Dynamic Duo Funhouse Escape
**SET NUMBERS:** 6857
**YEARS:** 2012

## DID YOU KNOW?
There have been three different LEGO Batcycles so far, as well as two-wheelers for Nightwing, Catwoman, and Bane.

Adjustable handlebars

Extra grip provided by chunky wheels

Rocket exhaust for bursts of speed

## ON TRACK
The Joker's funhouse includes a rollercoaster cart in colors matching Harley Quinn's costume. To date, it is the only LEGO DC Comics Super Heroes vehicle to run on tracks.

**Batman uses this Batcycle** to race to the rescue when the Riddler, the Joker, and Harley Quinn team up to trap Robin inside a funhouse filled with twisted traps! Its slim shape is perfect for dodging whatever the villains can throw at him.

# DRILL TANK
## UNDERWORLD UNDERMINER

## VITAL STATS

**OWNER:** Bane
**USED FOR:** Underground attacks
**GEAR:** Missile launchers, giant drill

**SET NAMES:** The Batcave
**SET NUMBERS:** 6860
**YEARS:** 2012

Lamp lights dark tunnels

Rotating drill carves through rock and earth

Missile ready to launch

## BIKE STRIKEBACK

Inside the Batcave, Batman uses his Batcycle to take on Bane's Drill Tank. It is similar to the Batcycle in The Dynamic Duo Funhouse Escape (set 6857), but has yellow wheels and missile launchers.

Six wheels turn the caterpillar tracks

**With its** tunnel-boring machinery at the front, Bane's Drill Tank is primed to mine its way into the Batcave for a surprise attack on Batman and Robin! The armored front also puts an impressive amount of space between the driver and his nemesis.

# SUPERMAN
## THE MAN OF STEEL

A determined face: Superman is ready to stand for truth and justice.

Eye-catching red cape

## DEFENDER OF METROPOLIS

On the other side of his double-sided face, Superman wears a confident smile—the Kryptonian enjoys banishing alien threats from his hometown, Metropolis.

Superman's yellow belt is also printed on his back.

**The last survivor** of the doomed planet Krypton, Superman was rocketed to Earth as a baby. Powered by the sun, the Man of Steel can fly faster than a speeding bullet, lift incredible weights, and fire lasers from his eyes.

# WONDER WOMAN
## *AMAZONIAN PRINCESS*

### VITAL STATS
.........................

**LIKES:** Honesty
**DISLIKES:** Lies
**FRIENDS:** Superman
**FOES:** Lex Luthor
**SKILLS:** Advanced fighting techniques
**GEAR:** Lasso of Truth

**SET NAME:** Superman vs Power Armor Lex
**SET NUMBER:** 6862
**YEAR:** 2012

The minifigure's hairpiece includes Wonder Woman's golden tiara.

Wonder Woman's costume is based upon the flag of the United States of America.

### FORCING THE TRUTH
No one can lie once they're tangled in Wonder Woman's Lasso of Truth. A turn of her head shows how angry she was to be captured by Lex Luthor.

**Born on Paradise Island,** Amazonian Princess Diana trained to be a warrior from the moment she could fight. The strongest woman on the planet, she now fights crime as a member of the Justice League.

# LEX LUTHOR
## SUPERMAN'S GREATEST ENEMY

### VITAL STATS

**LIKES:** Absolute power
**DISLIKES:** Anyone more powerful than himself
**FRIENDS:** None
**FOES:** Superman
**SKILLS:** An inventive mind
**GEAR:** Kryptonite gun

**SET NAME:** Superman vs Power Armor Lex
**SET NUMBER:** 6862
**YEAR:** 2012

A serious face as Lex plots Superman's downfall

No need for a hairpiece with this famously bald villain

A sharp business suit to wear to work at his company—LexCorp

### EVIL GENIUS

A master inventor, Lex Luthor designed and built a Kryptonite-powered battle armor to defeat Superman once and for all. The bait in his trap? None other than Wonder Woman herself!

**The Lex Luthor minifigure** was the first LEGO DC Comics Super Heroes villain not to come from Batman's rogues gallery. Instead, powerful billionaire Lex Luthor is Superman's arch nemesis in the city of Metropolis.

# LEX LUTHOR'S MEAN, GREEN MACHINE

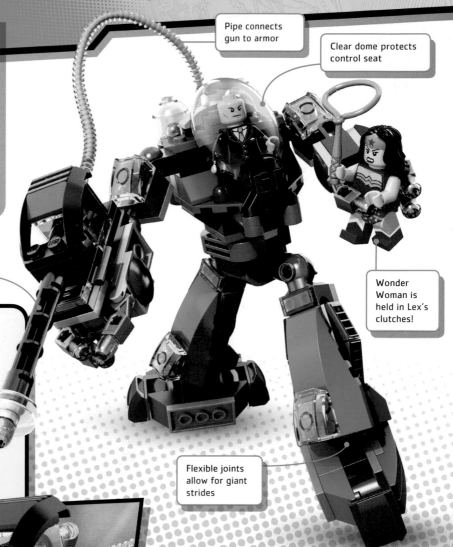

Pipe connects gun to armor

Clear dome protects control seat

Long gun barrel channels Kryptonite energy

Wonder Woman is held in Lex's clutches!

Flexible joints allow for giant strides

## ALL FINGERS AND THUMBS

A LEGO® Technic pin holds the gun in place on the armor's right arm. Both hands have moveable thumbs and two moveable fingers that can grasp minifigures and other objects.

**Lex Luthor** moved one big, mechanical step closer to catching Superman with this Kryptonite-powered robo-suit. Holding Wonder Woman prisoner, he plans to lure Superman into a trap and blast him with the mech's Kryptonite gun.

**LEX LUTHOR'S MECH**
Superman vs. Power Armor Mech (set 6862) allowed Lex Luthor to show off his technology skills in a big, green fighting machine. LEGO® Technic pins in the right arm turn his gun as he takes on two Super Heroes at once.

# LEX LUTHOR
## WICKED WARSUIT

## VITAL STATS

**LIKES:** Kryptonite
**DISLIKES:** Red-caped heroes
**FRIENDS:** None
**FOES:** Superman
**SKILLS:** Great intelligence
**GEAR:** The Deconstructor

**SET NAME:** Lex Luthor (polybag)
**SET NUMBER:** 30164
**YEAR:** 2012

This Luthor variant has a snarling face.

The warsuit follows Luthor's classic comic-book green and purple color-scheme.

Rocket packs allow Lex to fly like Superman

Remove the warsuit and you'll see a power-pack printed on the minifigure's chest.

## FEAR THE DECONSTRUCTOR!

One of Luthor's most despicable weapons, the Deconstructor can pull apart any LEGO object made of black bricks. Luckily Superman's costume is blue and red. Phew!

### DID YOU KNOW?

This exclusive Lex was given away at GameStop stores with pre-orders of LEGO *Batman 2: DC Super Heroes*.

**Realizing that he was** physically no match for Superman, Lex designed a powerful new armor, capable of flight and boosting his strength to super-human levels. He really will do anything to bring down the Man of Steel.

# BATMAN
## ELECTRO SUIT SHOCKER

### VITAL STATS
........................

**LIKES:** Gotham City
**DISLIKES:** Law-breaking
**FRIENDS:** Robin
**FOES:** Gotham City's criminal community
**SKILLS:** Delivering electric shocks
**GEAR:** Electro suit

**SET NAME:** DK's LEGO *DC Universe™ Super Heroes Batman™ Visual Dictionary* Exclusive
**SET NUMBER:** N/A
**YEAR:** 2012

### DID YOU KNOW?
The Electro suit made its first appearance in the LEGO *Batman 2: DC Super Heroes* video game.

No oval for the bat-symbol

A double-sided head also includes a smiling face on the other side

Light blue lines show where electricity can be generated

Taser points

### POWER POINTS
Without a cape, the taser points on the back of Batman's minifigure are clearly visible. Bruce designed the suit to release charges from both the front and rear. What a clever spark!

**Sometimes even Batman's** martial arts aren't enough to bring down Gotham City's super-villains. The Dark Knight's Electro suit amps up the action by delivering an electric shock with every punch.

## NO CLOWNING AROUND

### VITAL STATS

............................

**LIKES:** Being a grump
**DISLIKES:** Smiling
**FRIENDS:** The Joker
**FOES:** Batman
**SKILLS:** Helicopter pilot
**GEAR:** Laughing gas bomb

**SET NAME:** Batwing Battle Over Gotham City
**SET NUMBER:** 6863
**YEAR:** 2012

This henchman never fancies turning his frown upside down!

Lime green to match the Joker's vest

### BACK TO BASICS

There's no mistaking who this moaning minifigure works for. Not only are his clothes the Joker's trademark colors, but the Clown Prince of Crime's face is emblazoned on his back.

Black gloves leave no fingerprints

**The Joker's henchman** likes to crack safes but not smiles. This misery-guts is never happy. Maybe he doesn't like having his face painted. He'd better watch out, just in case the Joker gives him a dose of all that laughing gas!

# THE JOKER'S HELICOPTER

## TAKING A FUNNY TURN

### VITAL STATS

**OWNER:** The Joker
**USED FOR:** Laughing-gas attacks
**GEAR:** Missiles, laughing-gas

**SET NAME:** Batwing Battle Over Gotham City
**SET NUMBER:** 6863
**YEAR:** 2012

### DID YOU KNOW?

Set 6863 is an update of The Batwing: The Joker's Aerial Assault (set 7782) from 2006 (see p.26 and p.28).

"J" is for Joker

Toxic laughing-gas bomb

### HA-HA-HANG ON!

The Joker loves to show off, and can't help swinging on a rope ladder with a joke-shop gun while his henchman is left with the serious job of controlling the chopper.

Launchers for missiles—one on each side

**Uncharacteristically,** there are big grins all round the Joker's Helicopter. Both sides show the Joker's own sinister smile, while the bomb at the front has a fearsome leer. Needless to say, it's filled with laughing gas!

# BATWING
## FLIGHT AND FIGHT

## VITAL STATS
................................

**OWNER:** Batman
**USED FOR:** Flying like a bat
**GEAR:** Homing missile, rocket launchers

**SET NAMES:** Batwing Battle Over Gotham City
**SET NUMBERS:** 6863
**YEARS:** 2012

Rear wings can tilt up and down

Tail covers flaming exhaust

Front lights for night flying

## BACK BUTTON

Flipping up the cover behind the cockpit reveals a hidden button. Pressing it launches a homing missile that has Batarang-like wings, which is docked on the underside of the vessel.

Wings echoes Bat-symbol shape

### DID YOU KNOW?
The world's biggest bats can have wingspans of up to 170cm (5ft 6in).

**Batman is ready** to take on airborne enemies in his custom-built Batwing. It has rocket launchers hidden beneath its back wings and a homing missile under its tail, and is shaped like a bat so his opponents know who is coming for them!

# BATMOBILE
## GOOD LOOKS CATCH CROOKS!

### VITAL STATS
.........................

**OWNER:** Batman
**USED FOR:** Fighting crime, looking cool
**GEAR:** Missiles

**SET NAMES:** Batmobile and the Two-Face Chase
**SET NUMBERS:** 6864
**YEARS:** 2012

Batwings protect rear engine from side-on attacks

Twin missile launchers

Cooling stacks

Plush red interior has room for Batman in his cape

Vents draw air into engine at rear

### ARMS RACE

The Batmobile takes on a crane truck full of crooks when Two-Face and his henchmen raid a bank. Both cars fire super-fast missiles, but whose will hit their target first?

**The sleek curves** of the Batmobile hug the ground for a literal low profile—but the bright yellow wheels and flaming exhaust make for a pretty high-profile warning to crooks. Just one glimpse makes some of them quit crime altogether!

# TWO-FACE
## A MAN DIVIDED

### VITAL STATS
..........................

**LIKES:** The number 2
**DISLIKES:** The acid that caused his facial scarring
**FRIENDS:** Henchmen
**FOES:** Batman, bank guards
**SKILLS:** Bank robbery
**GEAR:** Lucky two-sided coin, dynamite

**SET NAMES:** The Batmobile and the Two-Face Chase
**SET NUMBERS:** 6864
**YEARS:** 2012

Scarred face

Dynamite is ready to blow.

The original 2006 Two-Face minifigure used a LEGO stud as a coin, but this variant has a printed round tile.

### MAKING HIS MIND UP
Two-Face made a bad decision when he stole a safe from Gotham City museum. Batman pursued and made sure the villain was soon laughing on the other side of his face.

Two-Face's split-color suit continues on the back of his minifigure.

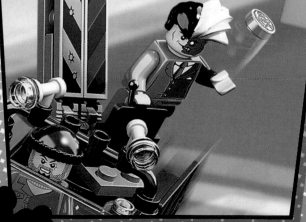

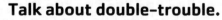

**Talk about double-trouble.**
Former District Attorney Harvey Dent still plans his crimes on the flip of his two-headed coin. This updated variant adds crazy color to his originally black and white wardrobe.

# GUARD
## BRAVE BANK EMPLOYEE

### VITAL STATS
..........................

**LIKES:** Standing guard
**DISLIKES:** Bank robbers
**FRIENDS:** Batman
**FOES:** Two-Face, henchmen
**SKILLS:** Brave and resourceful
**GEAR:** Walkie-talkie, handcuffs

**SET NAMES:** The Batmobile and The Two-Face Chase, Batman: Arkham Asylum Breakout
**SET NUMBERS:** 6860, 10937
**YEARS:** 2012, 2013

The Guard has the same face as the original 2006 Bruce Wayne minifigure.

LEGO handcuffs have appeared in more than 80 sets.

Guard uniform printing on torso.

### EMPLOYEE OF THE YEAR

Because of his brave actions at the Bank, the guard was offered a job at Arkham Asylum. Keeping a bunch of criminals in their cells? All in a day's work!

ARKHAM ASYLUM

**Most bank employees** turned and ran when Two-Face raided Gotham City bank. Not this guard. He raised the alarm and called Batman personally, standing ready to handcuff Harvey Dent and his heinous henchmen.

# HENCHMAN ONE

## HARVEY DENT'S RIGHT-HAND MAN

Cool shades: What every goon is wearing this season.

A similar color scheme to his notorious boss.

Torso printed with zips and studs.

### SAFE BREAK!

Henchman One only had one job on the raid on Gotham Bank—to make sure that the safe was safely hoisted clear. What a pity he forgot to shut the vault door!

**From an early age,** Henchman One knew he was destined to aid Gotham City's super-villains, and soon signed up to work with Two-Face. You can blame his mother. What kind of woman calls her son "Henchman One" anyway?

# HENCHMAN TWO

## HARVEY DENT'S LEFT-HAND MAN

### VITAL STATS
................................

**LIKES:** A good laugh
**DISLIKES:** Arkham Asylum
**FRIENDS:** Harley Quinn
**FOES:** Batman and Robin
**SKILLS:** Chemistry
**GEAR:** Remote control

**SET NAMES:** The Dynamic Duo Funhouse Escape, The Batcave
**SET NUMBERS:** 6857, 6860
**YEARS:** 2012

The mini pixie cap has appeared in more than 70 LEGO sets.

Villainous stubble and goatee combo.

Henchman Two wears the same jacket as his brother, Henchman One.

### GETAWAY DRIVER
The one thing Henchman Two can do better than his brother is making a clean getaway—except for that time he left Two-Face's car in a "No Parking" zone and got it towed away.

**Poor old Henchman Two** has spent his entire life in the shadow of his older twin brother. Henchman Two came a sorry second in every class at goon school, including Tying Up Guards, Blowing Up Safes, and Carrying Swag.

## IT'S GOT A DENT IN IT!

### VITAL STATS

**OWNER:** Two-Face
**USED FOR:** Robbing banks
**GEAR:** Crane, missiles, machine gun

**SET NAME:** Batmobile and the Two-Face Chase
**SET NUMBER:** 6864
**YEAR:** 2012

Bullet holes decorate car hood and crane

Two-Face stands at the crane controls

Stolen bank safe opens to reveal loot

Launcher for two missiles

Machine gun made from four LEGO binoculars pieces

### IT'S A STEAL!

The Batmobile and the Two-Face Chase set includes a bank building with a lever to knock out its windows, making it easy for Two-Face's crane to snatch the safe!

**Harvey Dent, aka Two-Face,** is causing trouble in his colorful crane car. Making his getaway after a bank robbery, he hopes some witnesses will say they saw a purple car leaving the scene, while others will swear it was orange!

# BIZARRO

## *SUPERMAN IN REVERSE*

## VITAL STATS

**LIKES:** Being bad
**DISLIKES:** Clark Kent
**FRIENDS:** The Bizarro League
**FOES:** Superman
**SKILLS:** Freezing vision and flaming breath
**GEAR:** Purple-blue flying cape

**SET NAME:** Bizarro
**SET NUMBER:** COMCON022
**YEAR:** 2012

### DID YOU KNOW?
In LEGO *Batman 3: Beyond Gotham* Bizarro stole Luthor's duplication ray to make Bizarro versions of the Justice League.

Chalk white and wrinkled skin

Reversed S-shield and muted colors

A medallion made of rock helps Bizarro remember his own name.

## BIZARRO BOTHER

The other side of Bizarro's head shows an even angrier face. The mixed-up minifigure was a San Diego Comic-Con exclusive, only available at the convention.

**Created by evil genius** Lex Luthor, this muddled clone of Superman gets everything the wrong way around. Childish and prone to throwing tantrums, Bizarro sees life in reverse. For him, good is bad and bad is good.

## VITAL STATS

**LIKES:** Being a hero
**DISLIKES:** Being a kid
**FRIENDS:** The Justice League
**FOES:** Black Adam
**SKILLS:** Magical abilities
**GEAR:** White cape

**SET NAME:** Shazam
(SDCC 2012 exclusive)
**SET NUMBER:** COMCON020
**YEAR:** 2012

### DID YOU KNOW?

Shazam appears in the LEGO *Batman 2: DC Comics Super Heroes* and LEGO *Batman 3: Beyond Gotham* video games.

Shazam shares a hairpiece with Bruce Wayne

Printed body emblazoned with lightning strike

Shazam wears one of the longest capes to appear on a LEGO DC Comics Super Heroes minifigure.

### RAGE AND FURY

Shazam uses his great wisdom to think his way out of trouble. That doesn't means he always remains calm. The other side of Shazam's head shows him shouting in anger.

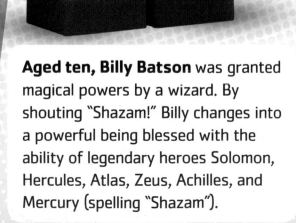

**Aged ten, Billy Batson** was granted magical powers by a wizard. By shouting "Shazam!" Billy changes into a powerful being blessed with the ability of legendary heroes Solomon, Hercules, Atlas, Zeus, Achilles, and Mercury (spelling "Shazam").

# JOR-EL
## SUPERMAN'S FATHER

## VITAL STATS
........................

**LIKES:** Science
**DISLIKES:** The Kryptonian Council
**FRIENDS:** His wife Lara
**FOES:** General Zod
**SKILLS:** Code imprinting
**GEAR:** Dark brown cape

**SET NAME:** Jor-El (polybag)
**SET NUMBER:** 5001623
**YEAR:** 2013

### DID YOU KNOW?
This minifigure is based on the 2013 *Man of Steel* movie. It was given free to customers at shop.LEGO.com and LEGO stores in June 2013.

Armor detailing is similar to Superman's *Man of Steel* variant

The "S" symbol means "hope" in Kryptonian.

### FROM FATHER TO SON
As "Clark Kent", Superman discovered a Kryptonian spaceship on Earth. From it, a holographic image of Jor-El appeared to teach Clark about his alien heritage and present the Last Son of Krypton with his Superman uniform.

While Superman's armor is gold in tones, Jor-El's is bronze.

**When chief scientist** Jor-El realized that his planet Krypton was about to explode, he tried to warn the Kryptonian High Council. With Jor-El's advice going ignored, he sent his son to Earth for safety. This son would become Superman!

# GREEN ARROW
## THE EMERALD ARCHER

Green hood

### DID YOU KNOW?
This is the only LEGO DC Comics Super Heroes Green Arrow minifigure not to have a bow and arrow!

Cool Super Hero stubble

Arrow insignia on belt

### TWO'S COMPANY
This rare Green Arrow kept company with black-suited Superman (see p.85) at the 2013 San Diego Comic-Con.

Kneepads printed on legs

**Another Comic-Con** exclusive, 200 Green Arrow minifigures were offered up for raffle in July 2013. They are based on Green Arrow's updated 2011 costume from the comics. Previously, Green Arrow had sported a yellow goatee.

# [redacted]

## SWOOPING SUPER HERO

### VITAL STATS

**LIKES:** Flying high
**DISLIKES:** Prison breakouts
**FRIENDS:** Robin
**FOES:** The Arkham Asylum inmates
**SKILLS:** Rounding up escapees
**GEAR:** Bat-wings, Batarang

**SET NAME:** Batman: Arkham Asylum Breakout
**SET NUMBER:** 10937
**YEAR:** 2013

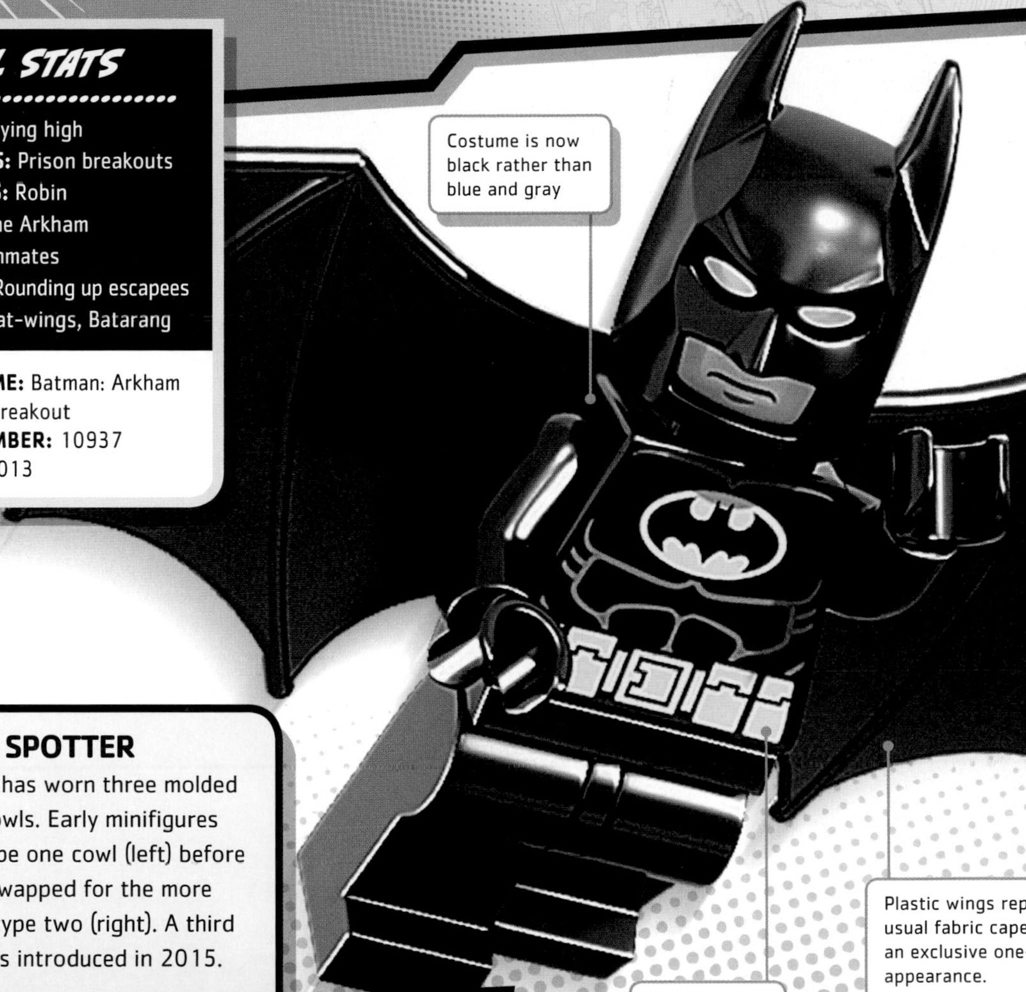

Costume is now black rather than blue and gray
Plastic wings replace usual fabric cape for an exclusive one-set appearance.
Utility Belt now contains pockets


### COWL SPOTTER

Batman has worn three molded LEGO cowls. Early minifigures wore type one cowl (left) before it was swapped for the more curved type two (right). A third cowl was introduced in 2015.

**This Batman** also appears, without his wings, in Batman Jetski (3016), Super Secret Police Dropship (70815), Batman: Man-Bat Attack (76011), The Batmobile and the Two-Face Chase (6864) and Batman: The Joker Steam Roller (76013) sets.

# THE JOKER
## ARKHAM PRISONER

The back of the minifigure is printed with Joker's Arkham Asylum inmate number—109370!

Same hair as the regular Joker variant

Bright orange Arkham jumpsuit

## PARTNERS IN CRIME

The doctors at Arkham Asylum hoped they could prepare the Joker for civilized law-abiding society, but the only thing the arch villain prepared behind bars were further crimes—especially with a certain Dr. Harleen Quinzel!

**Arkham Asylum** is the Joker's home away from home, although he never stays for long. Batman thought he had the Clown Prince of Crime under lock and key, until the dastardly villain slipped his restraints in the Arkham security van.

# HARLEEN QUINZEL
## LAUGHTER IS THE BEST MEDICINE

## VITAL STATS
........................

**LIKES:** Gag weapons
**DISLIKES:** Unrequited love
**FRIENDS:** The Joker,
Poison Ivy
**FOES:** Batman and Robin
**SKILLS:** Escapology
**GEAR:** Jester's hat

**SET NAME:** Batman: Arkham
Asylum Breakout
**SET NUMBER:** 10937
**YEAR:** 2013

### DID YOU KNOW?
Harley Quinn
first appeared in
a 1992 episode
of *Batman: The
Animated Series.*

A twist of Dr.
Quinzel's head
reveals Harley
Quinn on the
other side!

Doctor's outfit
comes complete
with name
badge clipped
onto front.

Harley's costume
is peeking out
from under her
doctor's uniform.

## MANIC MAKE-UP!
What every gal needs for a
quick change—Harleen has
a hidden make-up table at
Arkham, including a jester's hat
and a signed Joker pin-up!

**No one knew that** the Joker had
secretly persuaded psychiatrist
Harleen Quinzel to become the
villainous Harley Quinn. The double-
crossing doctor was then on hand to
help her puddin' to escape—along
with the rest of the inmates, too!

# ROBIN
## RED AND READY

## VITAL STATS
..............................
**LIKES:** Caged criminals
**DISLIKES:** Prison breakouts
**FRIENDS:** Batman
**FOES:** The Arkham
Asylum inmates
**SKILLS:** Recapturing criminals
**GEAR:** Kendo stick

**SET NAME:** Batman: Arkham
Asylum Breakout
**SET NUMBER:** 10937
**YEAR:** 2013

### DID YOU KNOW?
This minifigure is incredibly similar to the Robin in the *Batman: Arkham City* video game.

Hood to hide in the shadows

Two-sided head features a scared expression on the reverse.

Shorter cape worn for first time

Black gloves

### BETTER THAN A BROLLY
The Penguin better watch out—Robin is armed and dangerous. The monocle-wearing menace may have more than a few tricks up his umbrella, but they're no match for Robin's kendo stick!

**When Batman and Robin's** greatest enemies escaped Arkham Asylum, the Boy Wonder began the long task of bringing them all back to justice. This hooded variant swapped Robin's usual red legs for black to remain hidden for longer!

# ALL ABOARD FOR ARKHAM

## VITAL STATS
..........................

**OWNER:** Arkham Asylum
**USED FOR:** Prisoner transport
**GEAR:** Grill guard

**SET NAME:** Batman: Arkham Asylum Breakout
**SET NUMBER:** 10937
**YEAR:** 2012

Blue lights for use in an emergency

Room for one security guard

Arkham and Gotham City logos

## IN THE BACK
Double doors at the back of the van are wide enough to take in a lying-down Joker, his restraining frame, and his broad, maniacal grin. He couldn't possibly escape. Could he?

ARKHAM ASYLUM

GOTHAM CITY

28MB89

Protective grill guard

**This armored vehicle** serves as a prisoner transport for the most dangerous inmates of Arkham Asylum. The logo on the side lets citizens know they should steer clear, while blue lights on top flash as it speeds through the city!

# AQUAMAN
## RULER OF ATLANTIS

An angry face as Aquaman plans a retaliation attack.

Aquaman can blast water out of his trident.

Aquaman's muscles are also printed on the back of the minifigure.

## FROZEN FISH

The marine minifigure's reversible head shows a more somber expression. Aquaman had plenty of time to think when he was put on ice in Mr. Freeze's petrifying polar prison.

**Half-human and half-Atlantean,** Aquaman tirelessly defends Earth's oceans from attack. The briny ruler is able to communicate telepathically with fish and sea mammals, and was one of the founding members of the Justice League.

## IN POLE POSITION

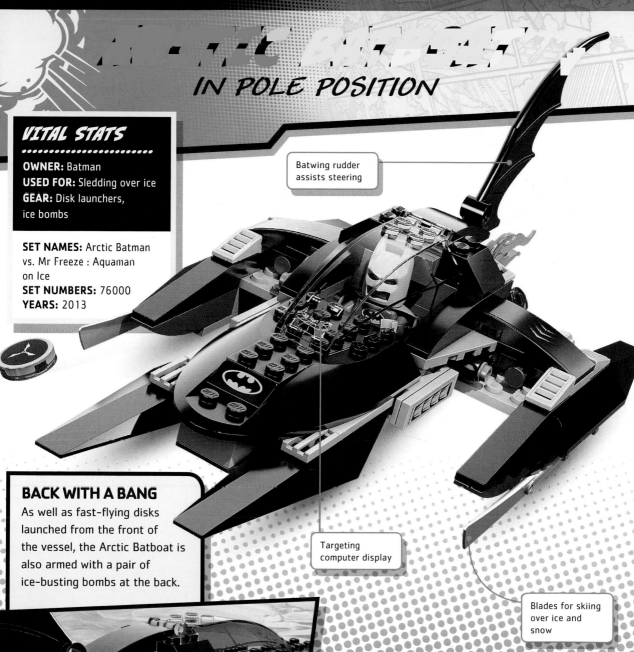

### VITAL STATS

**OWNER:** Batman
**USED FOR:** Sledding over ice
**GEAR:** Disk launchers,
ice bombs

**SET NAMES:** Arctic Batman
vs. Mr Freeze : Aquaman
on Ice
**SET NUMBERS:** 76000
**YEARS:** 2013

Batwing rudder
assists steering

Targeting
computer display

Blades for skiing
over ice and
snow

### BACK WITH A BANG

As well as fast-flying disks
launched from the front of
the vessel, the Arctic Batboat is
also armed with a pair of
ice-busting bombs at the back.

**Batman brings the heat** in his
Arctic Batboat! Designed to
withstand the coldest conditions, it
cuts across ice and snow at speed.
That makes it the perfect rescue
craft when Aquaman gets frozen in
a block of ice by Mr. Freeze.

# ARCTIC BATMAN
## A COLD KNIGHT

### VITAL STATS

**LIKES:** Saving his friends
**DISLIKES:** Being given the cold shoulder
**FRIENDS:** Aquaman
**FOES:** Mr. Freeze
**SKILLS:** Piloting the Batboat
**GEAR:** Batarangs

**SET NAMES:** Arctic Batman vs. Mr. Freeze: Aquaman on Ice
**SET NUMBERS:** 76000
**YEARS:** 2013

This minifigure uses the second version of Batman's LEGO cowl.

Bat-symbol in white and gray

White polar batsuit blends in with the snow.

### A COLD SENSE OF HUMOR

Batman isn't always the warmest character, but a twist of the hero's head reveals a less frosty side. Even in icy conditions, the Dark Knight keeps his cool!

**Available in just one** LEGO set, Arctic Batman charges to the coldest place on Earth to rescue Aquaman from the chilly clutches of Mr. Freeze. A camouflaged Caped Crusader will soon best the refrigerated rogue.

# MR. FREEZE
## STILL AS COLD AS ICE

### VITAL STATS

**LIKES:** Ice and snow
**DISLIKES:** Heat
**FRIENDS:** The Riddler
**FOES:** Batman, Aquaman
**SKILLS:** Cryogenics
**GEAR:** Freeze Gun

**SET NAMES:** Arctic Batman vs. Mr. Freeze: Aquaman on Ice
**SET NUMBERS:** 76000
**YEARS:** 2013

This minifigure variant's face features an all-new ferocious expression!

The Freeze Gun can encase anyone in a prison block of ice.

Air-conditioned wiring beneath Mr. Freeze's armor keeps him permanently chilled.

### FREEZE GUN

Mr. Freeze's 2013 Freeze Gun combines a LEGO plate piece with icy blue transparent pieces for freezing action. His bulky armor is suitably high-tech to match.

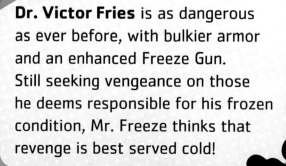

**Dr. Victor Fries** is as dangerous as ever before, with bulkier armor and an enhanced Freeze Gun. Still seeking vengeance on those he deems responsible for his frozen condition, Mr. Freeze thinks that revenge is best served cold!

79

# BATMAN
## THE BANE OF BANE

Black cowl covers double-sided head

Sharp-edged bat-symbol

Printed body armor

Complex bronze Utility Belt

### SAFE AND SOUND
Bane safely dispatched, Batman gives Gordon a lift back to police HQ in the Bat. Thanks to his alternate face, the Dark Knight looks happy to help out his old friend.

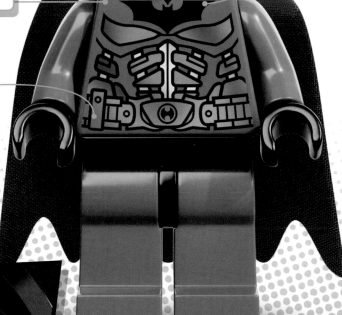

**When this armored** Batman spots Bane chasing down Commissioner Gordon in a stolen Tumbler, he swoops to the rescue in the Bat. This set is inspired by the 2012 *The Dark Knight Rises* movie.

# COMMISSIONER GORDON

## CHIEF OF GOTHAM CITY POLICE

### VITAL STATS
..........................

**LIKES:** Law and order
**DISLIKES:** Crime and deceit
**FRIENDS:** Batman
**FOES:** Bane
**SKILLS:** Keeping the peace
**GEAR:** Police handgun

**SET NAME:** The Bat vs. Bane: Tumbler Chase
**SET NUMBER:** 76001
**YEAR:** 2013

Being a cop in Gotham City is a scary job!

SWAT stands for Special Weapons Attack Team.

Police issue firearm

Can a bullet-proof vest *really* protect Gordon from villains like Bane?

### SWAT'S GOING ON?

Gordon may look scared but a twist of his head reveals a calm, determined face. Years of being the Gotham City chief of police have taken their toll. Just look at those bags under Jim's eyes!

**Unlike most of the** Gotham City police force, James Gordon is an honest cop. While Jim doesn't always approve of Batman's methods, he realizes that the Dark Knight is Gotham City's last hope against dangerous super-villains like Bane.

# BANE
## ROAD HOG

Bane's mask is gone, revealing a shaved head and his breathing apparatus.

**DID YOU KNOW?**
This minifigure is inspired by Bane in *The Dark Knight Rises* movie of 2012.

Printing shows bulletproof vest

On one hand Bane wears a glove, on the other... he doesn't.

### BULLETPROOF BACK
The back of Bane's 2013 minifigure shows more of his body armor while the straps that fix his breathing equipment to his bald head are clear.

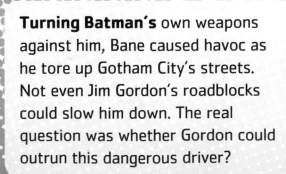

**Turning Batman's** own weapons against him, Bane caused havoc as he tore up Gotham City's streets. Not even Jim Gordon's roadblocks could slow him down. The real question was whether Gordon could outrun this dangerous driver?

## VILLAINOUS VEHICLE

## VITAL STATS

**OWNER:** Bane (stolen from Wayne Enterprises)
**USED FOR:** Menacing Gotham City
**GEAR:** Armor plating, missile launchers

**SET NAMES:** The Bat vs. Bane: Tumbler Chase
**SET NUMBERS:** 76001
**YEARS:** 2013

Hidden missile launchers

Bigger tires at rear

Design echoes Bane's scary mask

### UNDER THE ARMOR

Flipping up the armor plating above the back wheels reveals the Tumbler's secret weapon: two hidden missile launchers! A hatch in the top also flips open to reveal Bane inside.

**The first** time Bruce Wayne saw a Tumbler, he had it painted black and turned it into his Batmobile. When thuggish Bane stole one for himself, he kept it in its original desert camouflage colors. Some villains just have no sense of style!

# THE BAT
## ARMED AND DANGEROUS

### VITAL STATS

..........................

**OWNER:** Batman
**USED FOR:** Aerial pursuit
**GEAR:** Missiles, rescue rope

**SET NAME:** The Bat vs. Bane:
Tumbler Chase
**SET NUMBER:** 76001
**YEAR:** 2013

Click-joints allow the "arms" to stay in different positions

Flick-fire missiles on both arms

"Dark Knight"-style bat-symbol

Gordon holds on to the rescue rope

### ROOM FOR ONE MORE
The Bat has a second seat in the cockpit so that Gordon can fit behind Batman when he's finished hanging around. Propellers ensure the pair can speed away from Bane.

**Batman chases after Bane** and comes to Gordon's rescue in this experimental aircraft. Built by Wayne Enterprises, it is powered by propellers at the front and back, and is equipped with cannons and missiles on its two adjustable "arms."

# SUPERMAN
## THE MAN IN BLACK

**DID YOU KNOW?**
In the early 1990s, Superman wore a black costume with a chrome crest in the DC Comics books.

Distinctive curl

Silver S-Shield

Black outift signifies Superman's nightmare while captured in the Black Zero.

### COSTUME CHANGE

This exclusive figure is actually a black and silver variant of the 2013 *Man of Steel* minifigure, which was released to tie into the movie of the same name.

**It's the most** somber Superman of all and also one of the rarest LEGO DC Comics Super Heroes minifigures. Superman in his black costume was given away to just 200 lucky raffle winners at San Diego Comic-Con on 20 July 2013.

# LOIS LANE
## DAILY PLANET REPORTER

## VITAL STATS

..........................

**LIKES:** Following leads
**DISLIKES:** Being kidnapped
**FRIENDS:** Superman
**FOES:** General Zod
**SKILLS:** Investigating, escaping from aliens
**GEAR:** Wits and bravery

**SET NAMES:** Superman: Black Zero escape
**SET NUMBERS:** 76009
**YEARS:** 2013

### DID YOU KNOW?

This Lois Lane minifigure is based on her appearance in the 2013 *Man of Steel* movie.

Lois shares her long red hair with eight other minifigures.

Exclusive head only available on this minifigure.

Printed blouse and vest is suitable attire for a newshound.

### ESCAPE POD PERIL

Is it any wonder the other side of Lois' head has a terrified expression? She's been thrown out of General Zod's Black Zero ship in an escape pod!

Practical blue pants.

**Intrepid reporter** Lois Lane knew she had a story on her hands from the moment the first reports about Superman came in. Following her leads, she tracked the Man of Steel to his Smallville home and discovered his secret identity.

# SUPERMAN
## LAST SON OF KRYPTON

Peek beneath the cape and you'll see Superman's suit also printed on the back of the minifigure.

Silver armor detailing, as befits a battle-ready suit

### TURNING UP THE HEAT
One side of Superman's head shows an angry expression and red eyes as he fights to save Metropolis and Smallville from the villainous Zod. The other side wears a calmer frown.

Details of the suit are also printed on the legs.

**Darker than the** classic Superman outfit, this more modern-looking Man of Steel has rid himself of the red pants over his tights. This suit is modeled on traditional Kryptonian clothing, worn under battle armor on Superman's home planet.

# SUPER CAR
## METROPOLIS MOTOR

## VITAL STATS
.............................
**OWNER:** Unknown
**USED FOR:** Kryptonian weightlifting
**GEAR:** Hot yellow paint job

**SET NAME:** Superman: Metropolis Showdown
**SET NUMBER:** 76002
**YEAR:** 2013

### DID YOU KNOW?
The LEGO Group is the world's largest manufacturer of car tires—though only very small ones!

Handles allow a minifigure to hold onto the car

### NEED A LIFT?
This set also includes an antenna tower with a satellite dish, and a rubble ramp with a flip function to catapult the sports car—or the minifigures—into the air.

These tires appear in more than 200 LEGO sets

The car has room for a driver, but the set does not include one

**It's always a risk** parking your car in Metropolis. You never know when a superpowered showdown is going to turn it into just another piece of junk to be thrown around. At least the driver of this sports car isn't inside when General Zod picks it up!

# OFFROADER
## BIG IN SMALLVILLE

## VITAL STATS

**OWNER:** Colonel Hardy
**USED FOR:** Ground-to-air defense
**GEAR:** Missile launcher

**SET NAME:** Superman: Battle of Smallville
**SET NUMBER:** 76003
**YEAR:** 2013

### DID YOU KNOW?
Brick-yellow pieces such as the Offroader's cabin, were first seen in the LEGO® Adventurers theme in 1998.

Flick-fire missiles

Rocket launcher can rotate by 360 degrees

Cabin with two seats is one piece

## HARDY DEFENSE

Brave Colonel Hardy knows his Offroader's missile launcher is no match for General Zod's Black Zero Dropship (p.94), but he still uses it to defend Smallville when the Kryptonian criminal attacks.

Chunky all-terrain tires

**This sand-colored** utility vehicle is equipped for battle, with searchlights and a pair of rocket launchers mounted on the back. It can seat two U.S. Air Force soldiers, and is driven by Colonel Hardy when the town of Smallville comes under attack.

# GENERAL ZOD

## KRYPTONIAN CRIMINAL

### DID YOU KNOW?
A General Zod minifigure without his cape and helmet is available in Superman: Metropolis Showdown (set 76002).

Two-sided head featuring heat-vision eyes on the reverse

Black cape

General Zod's Kryptonian emblem

### SPACE ARMOR
Following Superman across the galaxy, Zod needs a Kryptonian battle helmet to breathe Earth's atmosphere. The aliens first clashed in the small town where Clark Kent, aka Superman, grew up—Smallville.

**As the Planet Krypton** ripped itself apart, Zod tried to overthrow the Kryptonian council and take control. Defeated, he and his co-conspirators were trapped in the Phantom Zone for all eternity—until Krypton's eventual destruction set them free!

# COLONEL HARDY
## U.S. AIR FORCE HERO

### VITAL STATS
..........................

**LIKES:** United States
Air Force
**DISLIKES:** Helicopters
**FRIENDS:** Superman,
Lois Lane
**FOES:** General Zod, Faora
**SKILLS:** Pilot
**GEAR:** Gun

**SET NAME:** Superman: Battle
of Smallville
**SET NUMBER:** 76003
**YEAR:** 2013

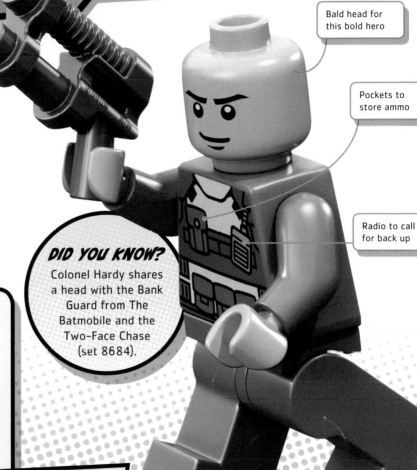

Bald head for
this bold hero

Pockets to
store ammo

Radio to call
for back up

### DID YOU KNOW?
Colonel Hardy shares
a head with the Bank
Guard from The
Batmobile and the
Two-Face Chase
(set 8684).

### GETTING THE DROP
ON ZOD

Colonel Hardy becomes a hero
when he stages an attack on
Zod's spacecraft. He triggers a
portal that drags the ship back to
the Phantom Zone proving that
the mighty Dropship (see p.94) is
no match for the nifty offroader.

**A member of the** U.S. Air Force,
Colonel Nathan Hardy was ordered to
bring down the battling Kryptonians
that were flattening Smallville.
However, the Colonel realized that
the Man of Steel wasn't their enemy
after Superman saved his life.

## VITAL STATS

**LIKES:** Explosions
**DISLIKES:** Jor-El and his family
**FRIENDS:** General Zod, Tor-An
**FOES:** Superman, Colonel Hardy
**SKILLS:** Hand-to-hand superpowered combat
**GEAR:** Helmet, Kryptonian gun

**SET NAME:** Superman: Battle of Smallville
**SET NUMBER:** 76003
**YEAR:** 2013

Faora also shares hair with Nightwing and Beast Boy.

Shock! Faora shares a two-sided head with Wonder Woman!

Faora's family crest

### SOLAR-POWERED

Like Zod, Faora needs breathing apparatus to survive Earth's atmosphere, but she soon discovers that the solar system's yellow sun grants her new superpowers of her own. She won't be needing her gun!

Hips printed on the minifigure's body

**To save Earth,** Superman surrendered himself to Zod. The triumphant General sent his second in command, Faora, to collect the Man of Steel and Lois Lane. Their encounter would lead to a devastating battle in Smallville.

# TOR-AN
## KRYPTONIAN SOLDIER

## VITAL STATS
**LIKES:** Fighting
**DISLIKES:** The Phantom Zone
**FRIENDS:** General Zod, Faora
**FOES:** Superman,
Colonel Hardy
**SKILLS:** Piloting the dropship
**GEAR:** Kryptonian gun

**SET NAME:** Superman: Battle of Smallville
**SET NUMBER:** 76003
**YEAR:** 2013

### DID YOU KNOW?
This minifigure has brown hair, just like his comic-book counterpart.

This minifigure has the same head as Lex Luthor.

Tor-An's Kryptonian emblem

No cape for this pilot—it would only restrict his space in the cockpit.

## TOO BAD, TOR-AN
As the pilot of the dropship, Tor-An sees all of the action from his domed cockpit. After the battle on Earth, he is banished to the Phantom Zone by Colonel Hardy.

**Tor-An helped** General Zod track Superman's path through the cosmos to Earth. Genetically engineered to be a soldier and a loyal member of the Kryptonian Warrior Guild, Tor-An is a master of several alien martial arts.

## ALIEN ATTACK CRAFT

### VITAL STATS
........................

**OWNER:** General Zod
**USED FOR:** Swooping down on unsuspecting planets
**GEAR:** Missiles, rotating cannon

**SET NAMES:** Superman: Battle of Smallville
**SET NUMBERS:** 76003
**YEARS:** 2013

Storage bays open to reveal weapons racks

Adjustable fins aid flight in atmosphere

Spring-loaded missiles hidden within hull

### DROPPED SHIP
The Dropship is designed to land on planets, and its fins can fold down to become feet that keep the weapons array raised above the ground.

Rotating cannon fires crackling energy bolts

**Criminal Kryptonians** General Zod, Faora, and Tor-An set out to destroy the town of Smallville in this superpowered spaceship! Only Superman can stop them, but he will have to dodge giant missiles and blasts of alien energy to do so!

# PLASTIC MAN
## THE STRETCHABLE SUPER HERO

Plastic Man
shares a
hairpiece with
Superman.

Those goggles
make Plastic Man
one cool dude—
or so he thinks!

### A QUICK CHANGE
Plastic Man's costume is
also printed on the back. The
outfit was inspired by Plastic
Man's updated appearance
in the 2011 Flashpoint event.
This was Plastic Man's first
appearance with tights, instead
of bare legs.

Boots
printed
on legs

**Given away** at U.S. GameStop
stores with pre-orders of LEGO
*Batman 3: Beyond Gotham,* this
exclusive minifigure gave super-
stretchy Patrick "Eel" O'Brian a
fantastic plastic form. Plastic Man
has the power to reshape his body.

**SMALLVILLE ATTACK**
Superman faces new alien foes in Superman: Battle over Smallville (set 76003) in a new costume design to resemble his look from the 2013 *Man of Steel* movie.

THIS IS "HARDY" A WALK IN THE PARK, HARDY HAR HAR!

# THE PENGUIN
## WRAPPED UP WARM FOR WINTER

## VITAL STATS

**LIKES:** Ice and Snow
**DISLIKES:** Heat
**FRIENDS:** The Riddler
**FOES:** Batman, Aquaman
**SKILLS:** Cryogenics
**GEAR:** Freeze Gun

**SET NAMES:** Batman: The Penguin Face Off
**SET NUMBERS:** 76010
**YEARS:** 2014

This variant still wears his monocle.

Newer umbrella has a brown handle.

### BIRD BRAINS
Constructed from simple LEGO bricks, these robot penguins stand guard around Penguin's stolen diamond. Their head design now comes with an attached bomb detonator, and the ice has turned their toes orange, rather than red (see p.16).

Fur edging perfect for chilly crimes.

**Talk about small man** syndrome. The Penguin still has smaller than average legs, but he makes up for it with one of the biggest egos in Gotham City. With this new fur-lined coat, he's also the winner of the best dressed super-villain award!

# SCUBA BATMAN

## DEEP-SEA DETECTIVE

Dark blue cowl accompanied by a scowl.

Harpoon gun at the ready.

Breathing apparatus leading to air tanks worn on the back.

Flippers for fast swimming action.

### TAKE A DEEP BREATH

Scuba Batman's alternate face sees the Dark Knight wearing his breathing apparatus. The Penguin will be in hot water when Batman reels him in for stealing Gotham City's gems.

**No villain** is safe from Batman—not even on the water. This deep-sea variant is ready to dive straight into the deep end with unique scuba gear printing on his body. It's a good thing his gadgets are all waterproof!

## NOT JUST FOR SPLASHING ABOUT

### VITAL STATS

**OWNER:** The Penguin
**USED FOR:** Brooding, hatching plans, bathtime
**GEAR:** Torpedo launchers

**SET NAME:** Batman: The Penguin Face Off
**SET NUMBER:** 76010
**YEAR:** 2014

Remote control operates robot penguins (see p.98)

Nice weather for ducks? Bring an umbrella!

Don't trust those big cute eyes...

Missiles hide under each wing (beneath the waterline)

### DUCK TAIL

This duck doesn't have any legs to paddle with, so it needs a propeller at the back to power it. The Penguin controls the craft from the steering wheel inside.

**Most people** are content with a rubber ducky in their bathtub, but the Penguin takes fowl play to a whole new level! His bright yellow bird is big enough to ride in and rules its watery roost with two feather-ruffling rockets. Duck!

### VITAL STATS
..........................

**OWNER:** Batman
**USED FOR:** Diving
**GEAR:** Torpedo launchers

**SET NAME:** Batman: The Penguin Face Off
**SET NUMBER:** 76010
**YEAR:** 2014

Batman in scuba gear

Harpoon gun

Clips to hold harpoon

Torpedo in flight

Fins steer left and right

### TWO BIRDS, ONE STONE

Batman uses his Scuba Vehicle to find a stolen diamond that is guarded by two of the Penguin's robot helpers.

**This solo speeder** dives down underwater so Batman can face his fishiest foes. It is small enough not to show up on enemy sensors, but is still effective, thanks to its twin torpedoes, powerful engine, and fishlike fins for steering.

## VITAL STATS

**LIKES:** Flying
**DISLIKES:** Explosives
**FRIENDS:** Batman
**FOES:** Man-Bat
**SKILLS:** Fighting, acrobatic circus tricks
**GEAR:** Grappling hook glider

**SET NAMES:** Batman: Man-Bat Attack
**SET NUMBERS:** 76011
**YEARS:** 2014

### DID YOU KNOW?

Nightwing's new black and red costume first appeared in the DC Comics in 2013.

Double-sided head shows expressions of smiling or grim concentration.

Black gloves protect hands when using glider.

The "V" of Nightwing's insignia continues on the back of his top.

## WINGED WONDER

Just like his mentor, Batman, Nightwing has plenty of cool vehicles. His rocket glider allows him to patrol the skies of Gotham City, keeping an eagle-eye out for trouble.

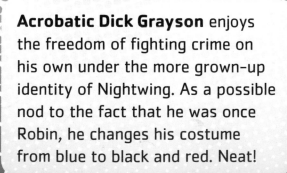

**Acrobatic Dick Grayson** enjoys the freedom of fighting crime on his own under the more grown-up identity of Nightwing. As a possible nod to the fact that he was once Robin, he changes his costume from blue to black and red. Neat!

# MAN-BAT
## GOTHAM CITY'S NIGHTMARE

### VITAL STATS
.........................

**LIKES:** Biology
**DISLIKES:** People who mumble
**FRIENDS:** Bruce Wayne
**FOES:** Batman, Nightwing
**SKILLS:** Sonar abilities
**GEAR:** Dynamite

**SET NAMES:** Batman: Man-Bat Attack
**SET NUMBERS:** 76011
**YEARS:** 2014

Man-Bat's headpiece hides an alternate worried face.

Fur printing continues on the back as well as the chest of Man-Bat's minifigure.

Extended batwings move with arms.

### GOING BATTY
Whenever Dr. Langstrom transforms into Man-Bat, he becomes a wild beast capable of dropping dynamite on the unsuspecting heads of Gotham City's citizens.

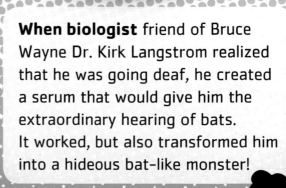

**When biologist** friend of Bruce Wayne Dr. Kirk Langstrom realized that he was going deaf, he created a serum that would give him the extraordinary hearing of bats. It worked, but also transformed him into a hideous bat-like monster!

# BATCOPTER
## A WHOLE NEW SPIN

**VITAL STATS**
........................

**OWNER:** Batman
**USED FOR:** Pest control
**GEAR:** Missiles, winch

**SET NAME:** Batman: The Riddler Chase
**SET NUMBER:** 76012
**YEAR:** 2014

Missile in launcher

Batwing-shaped tail fin

Jet engines on both sides

Missile in flight

## HOOKED!

Turning a gear at the back of the Batcopter lowers a hook on a rope. Turning the gear the other way reels in whatever—or whoever—the winch has hooked.

Flybars add stability

Winch can snare villains or rescue friends

**There's only room** for one Bat over Gotham City! So when the monstrous Man-Bat launches an aerial attack, Batman breaks out his brilliant Batcopter. If its weapons don't clip Man-Bat's wings, its winch will bring him down to earth!

# BATMOBILE
## WHEN SPEED'S THE NEED

### VITAL STATS
..........................

**OWNER:** Batman
**USED FOR:** Racing and chasing
**GEAR:** Hidden rockets

**SET NAME:** Batman: The Riddler Chase
**SET NUMBER:** 76012
**YEAR:** 2014

Twin exhausts

Adjustable rear wing for speed and defense

Downward-facing steering wheel

Bargeboards assist airflow for greater speed

## POCKET ROCKETS
The back of the Batmobile has a hidden weapon. The entire rear section rises up above the cockpit to become a cannon ready to fire a pair of rockets!

### DID YOU KNOW?
This Batmobile is inspired by the one that appears in the *Beware the Batman* animated series.

**With its low**, broad body and big, wide wheels, this Batmobile looks like a Formula 1 racing car. No wonder Batman uses it to keep up with his speedy Super Hero friend, The Flash—and with the villainous Riddler's own racing dragster.

# BATMAN
## BEWARE THIS BATMAN

### VITAL STATS
..........................
**LIKES:** His new Batmobile
**DISLIKES:** Bombing along
the road
**FRIENDS:** The Flash
**FOES:** The Riddler
**SKILLS:** Racing
**GEAR:** Batarang

**SET NAME:** Batman:
The Riddler Chase
**SET NUMBER:** 76012
**YEAR:** 2014

### DID YOU KNOW?
This outfit is based on
the 2013 animated
series Beware the
Batman, complete with
the show's distinctive
bat-symbol.

Costume
printing
continues on
the back

New style
bat-symbol

New high-tech,
bronzed Utility Belt
has curvier edges
than before.

### FACING HIS ENEMIES
Batman may have a sleek new
suit to go with a new Batmobile,
but this minifigure still shares
Batman's standard two-sided
head from earlier variants, plus,
of course, the trusty Batarang.

Gray gloves

**Batman debuted** a refined look as
well as a new set of wheels when he
had to take to the streets in a race
against the Riddler. Time to buckle
up with that shiny new Utility Belt
and hit the road in the Batmobile!

106

# THE FLASH
## THE FASTEST MAN ALIVE

Remove the helmet to find a two-sided face complete with a red mask surround.

Flip the head to reveal an angry expression

Exclusive helmet with yellow bolts on each side

Costume printing continues onto the back of the minifigure

Flash insignia

## THE NEED FOR SPEED

The Flash was on hand to help Batman chase down the Riddler's dragster. With his acrobatic abilities he jumps over the Riddler's bombs (and bananas), and remains in hot pursuit of the questionable criminal.

**DID YOU KNOW?**

The Flash appears in the LEGO *Batman 2: DC Comics Super Heroes* and LEGO *Batman 3: Beyond Gotham* video games.

**After he was struck** by lightning, police scientist Barry Allen developed the power to run at high speeds. Able to outrun anything on the planet, The Flash rushed into a life fighting crime and was one of the founding members of the Justice League.

# THE RIDDLER
## CRIME IN THE FAST LANE

### VITAL STATS
........................

**LIKES:** Anything green
**DISLIKES:** Red lights
**FRIENDS:** None
**FOES:** Batman, The Flash
**SKILLS:** Racing dragsters
**GEAR:** Question mark
cane, money

**SET NAME:** Batman:
The Riddler Chase
**SET NUMBER:** 76012
**YEAR:** 2014

New bowler hat
with purple
question mark

Purple driving
gloves

Exclusive green
jacket with question
mark motif

### BY HOOK OR BY CROOK
When not posing riddles, the
Riddler likes to rob banks and
drive away fast. He is even
armed with a question-mark
shaped crook to stop anyone
who tries to get in his way.

Two-tone
green on legs
and arms

**Unquestionably, the Riddler** is
one snappy dresser. From his new
racing green hat to his two-tone
legs, the peculiar villain is
committed to his theme: His back
features question marks galore and
the ends of a purple scarf.

## QUIZZY AND WHIZZY!

### VITAL STATS

**OWNER:** The Riddler
**USED FOR:** Quick getaways
**GEAR:** Bomb, moneybags

**SET NAME:** Batman:
The Riddler Chase
**SET NUMBER:** 76012
**YEAR:** 2014

Supercharged engine for extra speed

Flaming gas shoots from the exhaust pipes!

Riddler's question-mark symbol is decorated with flames

### CASHBACK!

The back of the Dragster features a spring-loaded mechanism to launch a bomb, plus a pair of moneybags stuffed with cash. These sacks can also be worn on the Riddler's back.

**Guess who** owns this ultra-fast dragster! The color and the repeated question mark can only mean the Riddler. He doesn't care who sees him race away from his latest bank robbery, however. He thinks he's far too fast to be caught.

# BATMAN OF ZUR-EN-ARRH

## THE ALIEN KNIGHT

BATMAN OF ZUR-EN-ARRH

## VITAL STATS

**LIKES:** Bright colors
**DISLIKES:** Shaving
**FRIENDS:** Batman
**FOES:** The criminals of Zur-En-Arrh
**SKILLS:** Hand-to-hand fighting
**GEAR:** Baseball bat

**SET NAME:** Batman of Zur-En-Arrh
**SET NUMBER:** SDCC036
**YEAR:** 2014

### DID YOU KNOW?

This version of the Caped Crusader first appeared in a 1940 Batman story called *The Superman of Planet X*.

Purple cowl

Two-sided face with stubble and growl on one side and smile on the other

Plain purple cape

## EXTRA-SPECIAL EXTRA-TERRESTRIAL

The alien Batman's garish colors continue on the minifigure's back. You can also see his yellow Utility Belt complete with pockets and Tiano's radio, capable of scrambling security systems.

**Alien scientist Tiano** spent years monitoring Earth. Impressed by Batman, Tiano become a cowled Caped Crusader for his home planet, Zur-En-Arrh. This colorful minifigure was an exclusive Comic-Con release.

## VITAL STATS

**LIKES:** Staying up late
**DISLIKES:** School nights
**FRIENDS:** Batman
**FOES:** Too many to mention
**SKILLS:** Acrobatics
**GEAR:** Grappling hook

**SET NAMES:** Batman Classic TV Series *Batmobile*, Batman: Defend the Batcave
**SET NUMBERS:** SDCC037, 10672
**YEAR:** 2014

Wide open yell

Unique head only available on this minifigure

Shorter yellow cape

### JUNIOR CRIME FIGHTER

Although this Boy Wonder was included as a San Diego Comic-Con exclusive, his true home is in this LEGO® Juniors set. Here he can be found working at his Robin-colored computer and leaping cheerfully off a building to come to Batman's aid!

Green legs adjoin separate red hip piece

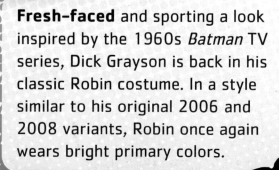

**Fresh-faced** and sporting a look inspired by the 1960s *Batman* TV series, Dick Grayson is back in his classic Robin costume. In a style similar to his original 2006 and 2008 variants, Robin once again wears bright primary colors.

# BATMAN
## EARLY KNIGHT

**VITAL STATS**
......................
**LIKES:** Helping young builders
**DISLIKES:** Complicated
instructions
**FRIENDS:** Robin
**FOES:** The Joker
**SKILLS:** Driving
**GEAR:** Batarang

**SET NAMES:** Batman Classic
TV Series *Batmobile*, Batman:
Defend the Batcave
**SET NUMBERS:** SDCC037,
10672
**YEAR:** 2014

A new light blue
cowl covers Batman's
two-sided head

Exclusive bright
blue cape only
found on this
Batman minifigure

Similar body print
to the 2012 Batman
minifigure

## TO THE BATCAVE...

Also starring as a San Diego
Comic-Con exclusive, this
Batman prefers the home
comforts of his LEGO Juniors
Batcave in set 10672. However,
he needs to fight off the Joker
before he can rest easy again...

**Available with a** LEGO Juniors set,
this Batman opts for a friendly
bright blue and gray costume.
Sticking with a simple theme, he
wears a streamlined Utility Belt and
a classic yellow bat-symbol.

# BATMOBILE
## RETRO ROCKET CAR

## VITAL STATS

**OWNER:** Batman
**USED FOR:** Crusading capers
**GEAR:** On-board computer

**SET NAME:** Batman Classic TV Series *Batmobile*
**SET NUMBER:** SDCC037
**YEAR:** 2014

Two front windshields

Light warns other road users to clear the way

Aerials transmit calls to the Batphone

Groovy red trim

## RARE RELEASE

This rare set was available only at the 2014 San Diego Comic-Con event. It came with Batman and Robin minifigures, and was released to mark 75 years of Batman adventures.

## DID YOU KNOW?

This set is based on the Batmobile from the 1960s *Batman* TV series.

**This unusual-looking** Batmobile has a separate seating compartment for both Batman and Robin. Powered by atomic batteries, it has a turbo-boosting rocket at the rear that blasts a jet of flame. Lucky there's a bright red warning light on the top!

# ROBIN
## THE SON OF BATMAN

Cross expression

Robin's shorter cape looks long on smaller Damian.

Short legs

### THE BRAT WONDER

Damian is small but has plenty of attitude. He immediately redesigned the Robin costume and insignia. But, as his alternate face shows, he's often shocked when his father puts him in his place.

**Damian is the son** of Bruce Wayne. Brought up by his assassin mother, Damian is a skilled, but extremely spoilt, child. On arriving in Gotham City he demanded that he take on the role of Robin. Tim Drake reluctantly stood aside.

# BATGIRL
## THE COMMISSIONER'S DAUGHTER

Double-sided head showing a smile and a frown

Cowl comes complete with red hair

Bright purple cape similar in design to Batman's cape

### GIRL POWER

At first Batman wasn't sure about Batgirl. But she soon proved her worth in fights with Gotham City's underworld—from the Joker's henchman to the Clown Prince of Crime himself. In a fight, her trusty Batarang is always by her side!

Torso printing displays a cheerful yellow bat-symbol

**Commissioner Gordon's** daughter Barbara had always been a Batman fan. She soon follows in the Dark Knight's footsteps, but she has to work hard to keep her identity secret from her detective dad.

## THE GRUMPY GOON

### VITAL STATS
..........................

**LIKES:** Destruction
**DISLIKES:** Smiling
**FRIENDS:** The Joker
**FOES:** Batman, Robin, Batgirl
**SKILLS:** Deconstruction
**GEAR:** Crowbar

**SET NAME:** Batman:
The Joker Steamroller
**SET NUMBER:** 76013
**YEAR:** 2014

Hard hat

Angry face shows through splotchy clown make-up

Orange construction vest is new and exclusive for this variant of the Joker's goon.

Tool of destruction

### A JOKER ORIGINAL
A quick glance at the henchman's back shows that the Joker has been busy customizing his goon's bright orange wardrobe. The fiend enjoys a play on words.

THE JOKER OF

**The Joker's right–hand** goon still hasn't cheered up. You would think that the miserable minifigure could at least manage a smirk. After all, he's been given free rein by his boss to demolish Gotham City. Some people are never happy.

# THE JOKER
## THE GIGGLING GANGSTER

## VITAL STATS
...........................

**LIKES:** Looking good
**DISLIKES:** Being scruffy
**FRIENDS:** His henchman
**FOES:** Batman, Robin, Batgirl
**SKILLS:** Causing devastation
**GEAR:** Popgun

**SET NAME:** Batman:
The Joker Steamroller
**SET NUMBER:** 76013
**YEAR:** 2014

### DID YOU KNOW?
This minifigure's design was inspired by the 1989 *Batman* movie.

LEGO fedora rarely seen in this purple hue.

Lopsided evil grin

The Joker also wears this lurid torso combination in Jokerland (set 76035).

## MONSTER MOTORS
It was no laughing matter when the Joker's Steam Roller carved a crazy path through Gotham City. But Joker's popgun couldn't save him from the combined might of Batman, Robin, and Batgirl.

**A criminal mastermind** can still take care of his appearance. This outrageous outfit betrays the Joker's gangster roots, adding a little sinister style to the proceedings. And of course, he's still smiling.

# THE JOKER'S STEAMROLLER

## DEVASTATINGLY FUNNY

Toothy
lipstick grin

Laughing-
gas bomb

## WHAT A GAS!

The Joker's laughing-
gas bombs are really laughing!
They have wicked grins, evil
eyes, big red clown's noses,
and can be fired from both
sides of the Steam Roller.

Joke gun with
"BANG!" flag

Roller crushes
everything in
its path.

**The jokes fall flat** when this
wild-looking wagon rolls into view.
It may have a massive grin on the
front, but there's nothing funny
about a demolition drive through
downtown Gotham City.

# BATWING
## A WING AND A SNARE

**VITAL STATS**
............................

**OWNER:** Batman
**USED FOR:** Surprise swoops
**GEAR:** Missiles, "attack mode" wings

**SET NAME:** Batman: The Joker Steam Roller
**SET NUMBER:** 76013
**YEAR:** 2014

Batman leans back in the streamlined cockpit.

Powerful jet engines

Two missiles on each wing

LEGO Technic elements allow the wings to move.

**GRAB AND GO**
When it switches to attack mode, the Batwing can bring its two wings together in a pincer movement to snatch unsuspecting villains up from the ground below!

**Every bat needs wings,** even Batman! This very special Batwing is equipped with four missiles and a surprise attack mode. It's the perfect choice to gain the advantage of height when the Joker takes to the streets with his Steam Roller.

# BATMAN
## DARK KNIGHT RISING

### VITAL STATS

**LIKES:** Armored vehicles
**DISLIKES:** Panic in the streets
**FRIENDS:** Jim Gordon
**FOES:** The Joker
**SKILLS:** Driving
**GEAR:** Batarang

**SET NAME:** The Tumbler
**SET NUMBER:** 76023
**YEAR:** 2014

Exclusive two-sided face not found on another Batman minifigure.

Unique, beefed-up armor

### DID YOU KNOW?

This minifigure is based on the costume worn by Batman in the movie *Batman Begins* and the first half of *The Dark Knight*.

Bronze Utility Belt

### READY TO TUMBLE

The other side of this minifigure's double-sided head shows a calm, considerate expression. Batman won't remain calm when he takes the Tumbler out on Gotham City's streets.

**It's the Darkest Knight** of all. After hanging up the cape and cowl, Bruce comes out of retirement as Batman. Gotham City is more dangerous than ever, meaning that his Batsuit is now more body armor than costume.

# THE JOKER
## THE DARK KNIGHT'S DARKEST VILLAIN

## VITAL STATS
..................

**LIKES:** Make-up
**DISLIKES:** Revealing his real face
**FRIENDS:** His goons
**FOES:** Batman
**SKILLS:** Causing chaos
**GEAR:** Just a winning smile

**SET NAME:** The Tumbler
**SET NUMBER:** 76023
**YEAR:** 2014

### DID YOU KNOW?
This minifigure is based on the Joker's appearance in the 2008 *The Dark Knight* movie.

Wide grin flashes yellow teeth

The Joker's face, hair, torso, and legs are all exclusive to this one set.

The Joker's torso displays four layers of clothing: a checked shirt, two vests, and a purple overcoat!

Wallet chain

### WILD SIDE
The alternate faces on this exclusive minifigure show two equally scary expressions. Added to this, the Joker's wild, scruffy hair is a far cry from his usual styled locks and the dark eye make-up further adds up to a sinister first impression.

**This minifigure of the Joker** has a natural skin tone smothered in chalk-white make-up and a painted on smile. But there's nothing funny about his terrible crimes. The Joker has never been so unpredictable. Batman had better watch out!

121

# TUMBLER
## ULTIMATE CRIME FIGHTER'S SERIES

Entry/exit by top hatch

Six flaps add drag for sudden stops

### DID YOU KNOW?
This Ultimate Collector's Series set is the largest LEGO DC Comics Super Heroes set to date, with 1,869 pieces.

These front tires are not found in any other set

Lights used when not in stealth mode

Hydraulic rods deploy attack mode

### COMPLETE CONTROLS
Two panels lift off the roof of the Tumbler to reveal an incredibly detailed cockpit, with two control panels, several display screens, steering controls, and a moving LEGO gear lever.

INTIMIDATE

**This feat of engineering** takes Batman's car collection to a whole new scale! Its huge tires provide traction, while its angular armor seems to go on forever. At the back, 1,500 horsepower blasts out via a giant jet turbine engine.

# SUPERBOY
## THE BOY OF STEEL

**DID YOU KNOW?**
Superboy's first LEGO appearance was in the videogame LEGO *Batman 2: DC Super Heroes*, where he wore an all-black outfit.

Same tousled hair as Robin (p.13)

Muscle tone shows through tight shirt

Rare two-tone minifigure arms gives t-shirt effect

### A LIKELY LAD

In 2015 exclusive set 5004077 revealed another Super Hero from faraway: Lightning Lad. This character's ability to create eletricity is shown with the dramatic lightning bolts on his minifigure's torso and legs.

Blue jeans show Superboy's casual approach to costumes!

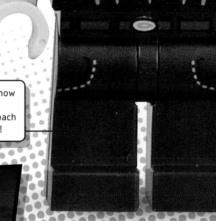

**Conner Kent** was cloned from Lex Luthor and Superman's DNA, but still became Superman's pal, earning the Kryptonian name Kon-El. He has similar abilities to Superman, such as super strength, heat vision, x-ray vision, freeze breath, and flight.

# GREEN LANTERN
## GUARDIAN OF EARTH

### VITAL STATS

**LIKES:** Protecting the Earth
**DISLIKES:** Losing his Lantern
**FRIENDS:** Batman
**FOES:** Sinestro
**SKILLS:** Space flight
**GEAR:** Green Lantern

**SET NAME:** Green Lantern vs. Sinestro
**SET NUMBER:** 76025
**YEAR:** 2015

Green Lantern shares a hairpiece with Commissioner Gordon.

A two-sided head features a grinning face on the reverse

Green Lantern uniform complete with the insignia of the Lantern Corps

### DOWN-TO-EARTH

An earlier Green Lantern, based on the 2011 *Green Lantern* movie, was given away to 1,500 raffle winners at the 2011 San Diego Comic-Con, with a smaller quantity released at New York Comic Con the same year.

Black and green printing continues on the back.

**When test pilot** Hal Jordan discovered the wreckage of an alien spacecraft he received a power ring that transformed him into the Green Lantern. Drawing power from his cosmic lantern, Hal protects the solar system from attack.

# SINESTRO
## FALLEN LANTERN

### VITAL STATS
...........................

**LIKES:** Absolute power
**DISLIKES:** Hal Jordan
**FRIENDS:** The Sinestro Corps
**FOES:** Green Lantern, Batman
**SKILLS:** Lantern-napping
**GEAR:** Power staff

**SET NAME:** Green Lantern vs Sinestro
**SET NUMBER:** 76025
**YEAR:** 2015

Double-sided head with a snarling face on the back

Uniquely bright pink face

Symbol of the Sinestro Corps

Yellow and black printing continues on the back of the minifigure.

## LANTERN LIFT–OFF
Sinestro stole Hal Jordan's Lantern and placed it within a protective cage on his home planet of Korugar. It has just enough space for one object—either the Lantern or Sinestro himself!

**Once considered the** greatest Green Lantern of them all, Sinestro was actually using his great powers to enslave alien races. Stripped of his power ring, Sinestro formed the evil Sinestro Corps and became the Green Lantern's sworn enemy.

# SPACE BATMAN

## COSMIC CAPED CRUSADER

## VITAL STATS

**LIKES:** Exploring
**DISLIKES:** Extra-terrestrial thieves
**FRIENDS:** Green Lantern
**FOES:** Sinestro
**SKILLS:** Space flight
**GEAR:** Extending wings

**SET NAME:** Green Lantern vs. Sinestro
**SET NUMBER:** 76025
**YEAR:** 2015

Silver cowl with shorter ears

Wings in closed formation

Air tubes for breathing in space

Space suit printed on both sides of body

Silver arms and legs

## SPACE FLIGHT

The Space Batman variant comes with two translucent plastic capes. Remove Batman's rocket pack to switch over to the outstretched bat-wings and take flight after Sinestro.

**In space,** two heads are better than one. The first is printed with a special visor and breathing apparatus, while this Cosmic Caped Crusader variant also comes with a separate, standard two-sided head.

# GREEN LANTERN JET

## IMAGINE THAT!

### DID YOU KNOW?

Green Lantern can use his power ring to make solid constructs of anything he imagines—not just spaceships!

Shooters on both wings

Forward shooters

### A GIANT LEAP...

The Green Lantern vs. Sinestro set also comes with a special Super Jumper piece that serves as a springboard for minifigures to perform giant leaps.

**Made from energy** channeled through a power ring, this spaceship only works while Green Lantern is concentrating! Hal Jordan creates it to chase after Sinestro, when the villain steals his Power Battery and takes it to the planet Korugar.

# WONDER WOMAN

## AMAZONIAN WARRIOR

### VITAL STATS
..................

**LIKES:** Making a monkey of villains
**DISLIKES:** Bananas
**FRIENDS:** Batman, the Flash
**FOES:** Gorilla Grodd, Captain Cold
**SKILLS:** Piloting invisible jet planes
**GEAR:** Swords

**SET NAME:** Gorilla Grodd Goes Bananas
**SET NUMBER:** 76026
**YEAR:** 2015

Face printing appears in six other sets

Silver tiara

New battle-ready uniform exclusive to set

Pants replace her satin tights

### SWORD HELD HIGH
A twist of Wonder Woman's head reveals her scowling as she rushes into the fray, armed with her Amazonian sword. She's a foe to be reckoned with thanks to a lifetime of combat training.

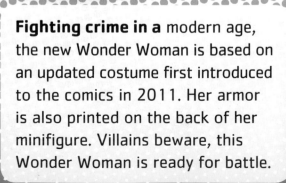

**Fighting crime in a** modern age, the new Wonder Woman is based on an updated costume first introduced to the comics in 2011. Her armor is also printed on the back of her minifigure. Villains beware, this Wonder Woman is ready for battle.

# NOTHING TO SEE HERE!

## VITAL STATS

**OWNER:** Wonder Woman
**USED FOR:** Stealth missions
**GEAR:** Shooters, supersonic engine

**SET NAME:** Gorilla Grodd Goes Bananas
**SET NUMBER:** 76026
**YEAR:** 2015

### DID YOU KNOW?
Wonder Woman's Invisible Jet can also travel into outer space—but only for short periods of time.

Hinged cockpit canopy

Transparent blue shooter

Missile launcher without shooter

Unique transparent wing pieces

## GORILLA TACTICS
Wonder Woman uses her Invisible Jet to come to the rescue of a Truck Driver (p.133) in the Gorilla Grodd Goes Bananas set. The driver probably wishes he was invisible, too!

**Wonder Woman built** the Invisible Jet in the name of peace. By traveling unseen, she can carry out her missions without starting a fight. The plane is super-fast and a complete stealth vehicle. Even the exhaust flames are invisible!

# BATMAN
## NEW KNIGHT

## VITAL STATS
........................

**LIKES:** New technology
**DISLIKES:** Low morals
**FRIENDS:** Wonder Woman,
The Flash
**FOES:** Gorilla Grodd,
Captain Cold
**SKILLS:** Piloting his Bat-Mech
**GEAR:** Batarang

**SET NAMES:** Gorilla Grodd
Goes Bananas, Batboat
Harbor Pursuit
**SET NUMBERS:** 76026,
76034
**YEAR:** 2015

Cape made from new
fabric material

New chinless black
cowl similar to
Batman's space
suit helmet

Body armor
with larger black
bat-symbol

Two-sided head

## BOOT-LEGGER BATMAN
The Batman minifigure from
Jokerland (set 76035) is the
only variant to feature a pair
of boots. Complete with a dark
gray suit and golden Utility Belt,
he is ready to take the Gotham
City underworld by storm!

**Like Wonder Woman,** this Batman
minifigure is based on new costume
designs first introduced to the
comics in 2011. Batman now wears
detailed body armor printed on the
front and back of the minifigure.

# CAPTAIN COLD

## HOODED HOODLUM

Protective hood

Coolly confident grin

Warm parka printing on both sides of the minifigure

### VITAL STATS

**LIKES:** Cold
**DISLIKES:** Heat
**FRIENDS:** Gorilla Grodd
**FOES:** The Flash, Batman, Wonder Woman
**SKILLS:** Turning down the heat
**GEAR:** Ice shooter

**SET NAME:** Gorilla Grodd Goes Bananas
**SET NUMBER:** 76026
**YEAR:** 2015

## CHILLED TO THE BONE

Captain Cold's alternate face shows his features frozen into a frown. Perhaps facing the Batman wasn't the best idea—after all, the Caped Crusader has plenty of icy experience with Mr. Freeze!

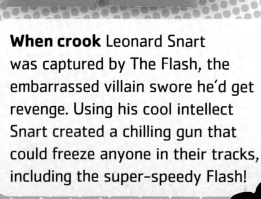

**When crook** Leonard Snart was captured by The Flash, the embarrassed villain swore he'd get revenge. Using his cool intellect Snart created a chilling gun that could freeze anyone in their tracks, including the super-speedy Flash!

# GORILLA GRODD
## GOING APE

## VITAL STATS
..............................

**LIKES:** Bananas
**DISLIKES:** Rotten fruit
**FRIENDS:** Captain Cold
**FOES:** The Flash, Batman, Wonder Woman
**SKILLS:** Mind control
**GEAR:** Banana

**SET NAME:** Gorilla Grodd Goes Bananas
**SET NUMBER:** 76026
**YEAR:** 2015

Mind control equipment

## JUST BANANAS

If there's one thing Gorilla Grodd loves, it's trying to take over the world. But if there's another thing he loves, it's nice tasty bananas. So much so that he attacks this unsuspecting truck driver.

**Once Grodd was just** another gorilla living in a rainforest. That was until a crashed alien spacecraft gave the great ape hyper-intelligence. Now Grodd is able to telepathically control minds!

# TRUCK DRIVER
## DRIVEN AROUND THE BEND

## VITAL STATS

**LIKES:** Delivering fruit
**DISLIKES:** Angry customers, telepathic gorillas
**FRIENDS:** Batman, the Flash, Wonder Woman
**FOES:** Gorilla Grodd
**SKILLS:** Driving
**GEAR:** Bananas

**SET NAME:** Gorilla Grodd Goes Bananas
**SET NUMBER:** 76026
**YEAR:** 2015

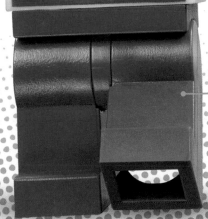

Terrified expression

Back printing shows that this driver works for "Banana Co."

Happy banana logo

Practical dungarees

## A BAD DAY AT WORK

First his truck is raided, then he's swung upside-down by a very hungry Grodd! It's shaping up to be a bad day for the truck driver. Frequent super-villain attacks mean there are lots of job vacancies in Gotham City as workers flee from danger.

**Talk about being** in the wrong place at the wrong time. All the Truck Driver had to do was deliver a batch of bright yellow bananas to Gotham City's fruit lovers. Easy—unless you run into a giant hyper-intelligent gorilla.

# BAT-MECH
## DESTINED FOR BIG THINGS

### VITAL STATS

**OWNER:** Batman
**USED FOR:** Standing up to bad guys
**GEAR:** Net shooter

**SET NAME:** Gorilla Grodd Goes Bananas
**SET NUMBER:** 76026
**YEAR:** 2015

Batman at the controls

Arms can move in all directions

Wing armor

Net-shooter arm

Twin stud shooters

Broad feet for balance

A rare LEGO thumb!

## NET-WORKING

Batman can catch criminals with one hand using his Bat-Mech! The vehicle's right hand is a cannon containing a net that flies out to ensnare villains at the touch of a button. On this occasion, The Flash came along to help rope up Grodd, too.

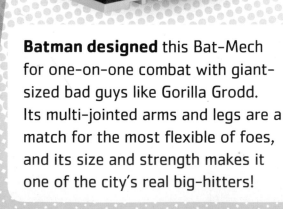

**Batman designed** this Bat-Mech for one-on-one combat with giant-sized bad guys like Gorilla Grodd. Its multi-jointed arms and legs are a match for the most flexible of foes, and its size and strength makes it one of the city's real big-hitters!

# SEA SAUCER
## FISH DISH

**OWNER:** Black Manta
**USED FOR:** Underwater villainy
**GEAR:** Torpedo launchers

**SET NAME:** Black Manta Deep Sea Strike
**SET NUMBER:** 76027
**YEAR:** 2015

Propeller keeps sub moving

The cockpit even has room for a minifigure with a big helmet!

Torpedo launcher

## MEGA BITE

Think sharks are scary? Wait until you see this roboshark! Armed with laser shooters on both sides, the swimming cyborg is controlled by Black Manta from inside his Sea Saucer.

Black Manta symbol

**Roguish Black Manta** wants to rule the oceans from this stealthy submarine. He uses it to take Robin prisoner in the ruined underwater world of Atlantis, and fires its torpedos at Batman and Aquaman when they launch a rescue attempt.

# BLACK MANTA
## DEEP-SEA DANGER

## VITAL STATS

**LIKES:** Fishing
**DISLIKES:** The sea
**FRIENDS:** None
**FOES:** Aquaman, Batman
**SKILLS:** Deep-sea diving
**GEAR:** Spear, Torpedo-toting robo-shark

**SET NAME:** Black Manta Deep Sea Strike
**SET NUMBER:** 76027
**YEAR:** 2015

There's no minifigure head beneath that oversized helmet.

Tubes take air into the helmet

## SUPER SUIT

Although Black Manta has no superpowers, he's a formidable foe. His custom-made scuba suit can survive the extreme pressure of the seabed, fire lasers from his eyes, and shoot electric bolts. He's also armed with a spear for closer attacks.

Scuba suit printing continues on the back

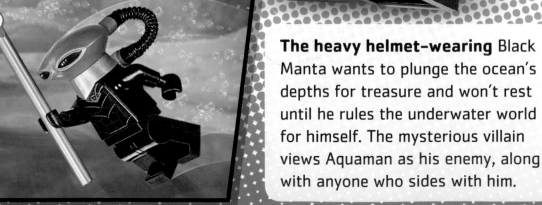

**The heavy helmet–wearing** Black Manta wants to plunge the ocean's depths for treasure and won't rest until he rules the underwater world for himself. The mysterious villain views Aquaman as his enemy, along with anyone who sides with him.

# SUBMARINE SIDEKICK

Under the goggles, this side of Robin's face reveals printed-on scuba gear.

Yellow air-tank attached around neck

## DID YOU KNOW?

This minifigure also comes with a black hairpiece for when you remove Robin's helmet.

## UNDERWATER PRISON

No wonder a twist of Robin's head reveals a scared expression. Not only does Black Manta slap-on the handcuffs, he also attaches a chain to Robin's legs to anchor him to the seabed.

Flippers attach directly to feet

**Robin was enjoying** a quick dip beneath the waves when Black Manta clapped him in chains and whisked him away in his sinister Sea Saucer. Robin's crime-fighting career has never sunk so low, but he is at least dressed for the occasion.

# BATMAN
## BACK UNDERWATER

Uses a similar double-sided head to the previous Scuba minifigure

A newer softer cape

### TEST DIVE
Even though Black Manta abducting the Boy Wonder is annoying, it does give Batman a chance to test the brand new Bat Sub. Not all bad, then!

**With the same body** as the Jokerland Batman, this deep-sea Detective also uses a revised cowl. The new helmet doesn't include a chin guard, so there's printing of the mask on Batman's head itself.

# BAT-SUB
## DOUBLE DIVER

Rudder turns to steer sub

Mini sub docks here

**DID YOU KNOW?**

Scuba stands for "self-contained underwater breathing apparatus."

**VITAL STATS**
................................

**OWNER:** Batman
**USED FOR:** Deep-sea missions
**GEAR:** Mini sub, torpedoes

**SET NAME:** Black Manta Deep Sea Strike
**SET NUMBER:** 76027
**YEAR:** 2015

Torpedo launcher

Wheel to open engine compartment

## SECONDARY SUB

Dressed in his scuba gear, Robin powers through the water by holding onto the back of this mini sub. When not in use, it connects to the main Bat Sub.

Engine heat vent

**More like a shark** than a bat, this long, slim sub slices through water at high speed, in search of its prey: the villainous Black Manta! It is actually two underwater vehicles in one, with a small, detachable glider docked at the back.

# GREEN ARROW

## ANGRY ARCHER

Face stubble printing reveals that the Green Archer is in need of a shave.

Green plastic hood hangs from around the neck.

### ARMED AND DANGEROUS

You can swivel the Green Arrow's head to reveal an angry expression. A quiver full of arrows is also printed on the back of his torso, beneath his cape.

Standard LEGO bow and arrow in green.

**With a body similar** to the earlier San Diego Comic-Con exclusive, this Green Arrow has plain green legs rather than kneepads. Luckily for the Justice League, the Arrow stays on target no matter what his workday wardrobe.

# THE JUSTIC LEAGUE'S SPACESHIP

## DID YOU KNOW?
Darkseid Invasion was the first set to include a springy Super Jumper element—hidden in the Javelin's cargo bay.

Double doors open to reveal large cargo bay

Justice League emblem on nose cone

A lever can tilt the wing tips upwards for landing.

There is room inside the cockpit for Green Arrow's bow alongside the archer.

## JAW-DROPPING
The underside of the Javelin has two rocket launchers and a bomb door that opens like a jaw to drop its cargo—or to scoop up an enemy minifigure!

**Green Arrow** flies this sleek Justice League jet, which can travel through air, underwater, or in the vacuum of space. It was built by Batman and is equipped with all the gadgets and gear you'd expect from him—just not in his usual dark color scheme!

# DARKSEID
## OVERSIZED ALIEN OVERLORD

Cracked gray skin

Darkseid's red eyes can launch laser beams.

Huge gripping hand

## CANNONBALL CHAOS

Darkseid's invasion starts in Metropolis, when the alien overlord plays skittles with skyscrapers, blasting cannonballs from a Hover Launcher enlarged for his oversized form.

**The tyrannical ruler** of Apokolips has set his eyes on the rest of the universe. Invulnerable to anything but his own eye-beams, Darkseid is super-strong and resourceful. Nothing will stop his takeover plans.

# HAWKMAN
## WINGED WARRIOR

## VITAL STATS

**LIKES:** Flying high
**DISLIKES:** Having his wings clipped
**FRIENDS:** Superman, Cyborg, Green Arrow
**FOES:** Darkseid
**SKILLS:** Flight
**GEAR:** Wings, Mace

**SET NAMES:** Darkseid Invasion
**SET NUMBERS:** 76028
**YEARS:** 2015

Wings attach to Hawkman's minifigure using gold studs.

## BEATING WINGS

Hawkman comes with two interchangeable set of plastic wings, one spread out for flight and the other drawn in for fight! There's also a two-sided head beneath that helmet.

Hawk symbol joins crossing chest straps.

**Archaeologist Carter Hall** uses magical Nth Metal to soar through the air as the savage Hawkman. This Justice League member is no young featherweight—he's actually a reincarnated Egyptian prince!

# CYBORG
## MECHANICAL WHIZZ

## VITAL STATS
......................................

**LIKES:** Justice League
**DISLIKES:** Rusty parts
**FRIENDS:** Superman, Green
Arrow, Hawkman, Beast Boy
**FOES:** Darkseid
**SKILLS:** Cybernetic attacks
**GEAR:** Stud Shooter

**SET NAMES:** Darkseid
Invasion
**SET NUMBERS:** 76028
**YEARS:** 2015

Stud Shooter keeps
villains at bay.

Snarling face partially
covered by Cyborg's
cybernetic helmet.

## METALLIC MAGNETISM
In the Justice League, Cyborg
uses his varied skills to fend off
many villains, including Brainiac.
In LEGO *Batman 2: DC Super
Heroes* Cyborg temporarily has
useful magnetic powers!

Leg printing
reveals extensive
metallic parts.

**When Vic Stone** was injured, his
father rebuilt him as half-man, half-
machine. Becoming Cyborg, he can
interface with computers, although
rumors that he uses his advanced
cybernetics to cheat while playing
Batman at video games aren't true!

# HOVER DESTROYER
## DARKSEID'S HOVERBOARD

## VITAL STATS

**OWNER:** Darkseid
**USED FOR:** Fighting flying Super Heroes
**GEAR:** Omega cannon

**SET NAMES:** Darkseid Invasion
**SET NUMBERS:** 76028
**YEARS:** 2015

Large levers for Darkseid's huge hands

Bright red balls of Omega energy are launched from this cannon.

Space to store second cannonball behind launcher

Omega symbol on front of craft

## BALANCING ACT

Darkseid positions his brawny bulk at the back of the Hover Destroyer, standing on special footholds. From this secure stance he takes on a full cohort of Superman, Green Arrow, Cyborg, and Hawkman.

**Darkseid can match** Superman with many alien powers, but one thing that he can't do is fly! It takes three anti-gravity discs to lift the muscular monster on this floating weapons platform, along with his heavy, high-tech cannon.

# SUPERMAN
## FLYING TO THE RESCUE

## VITAL STATS
••••••••••••••••••••

**LIKES:** Working with his cousin
**DISLIKES:** Alien invasions
**FRIENDS:** Supergirl,
Martian Manhunter
**FOES:** Brainiac
**SKILLS:** Leaping tall buildings
in a single bound
**GEAR:** Cape

**SET NAME:** Brainiac Attack
**SET NUMBER:** 76040
**YEAR:** 2015

### DID YOU KNOW?
The minifigure from
Superman vs. Power
Armor Lex also dons
the new cape for the
2015 San Diego
Comic-Con set.

Red eyes
ready to blast
heat vision

## SUPER-SWITCHEROO
There's more mix-and-match Man
of Steel with Darkseid Invasion
(set 76028) as the Superman in
this set includes a body and
head from Superman vs. Power
Armor Lex (set 6862) plus the
new cape. Phew!

**This mixed-up minifigure's** body
was originally found in Superman
vs. Power Armor Lex (set 6862),
while his head comes from the
*Man of Steel* movie set. The cape
is brand new however, made from
a new softer, stretchier material.

## VITAL STATS

**LIKES:** Flying into action
**DISLIKES:** Rules
**FRIENDS:** Superman, Martian Manhunter
**FOES:** Brainiac
**SKILLS:** Heat vision, super-strength
**GEAR:** Cape

**SET NAME:** Brainiac Attack
**SET NUMBER:** 76040
**YEAR:** 2015

### DID YOU KNOW?

Supergirl made her first appearance in a 1959 issue of *Action Comics*.

Long flowing blond hair

### CROSS KRYPTONIAN

Don't be fooled by Supergirl's calm face—the other side reveals an angry expression and heat-vision eyes. Supergirl shares Superman's power, but she doesn't share his self-restraint and mild-mannered nature!

Supergirl's torso has been adjusted especially for her, and is exclusive to this variant.

**What do you get** when you cross superpowers with teenage attitude? Plenty of trouble, that's what! Sent to Earth to care for her cousin Kal-El, Kara Zor-El's spacecraft was knocked off course. She actually arrives years after Superman had grown up!

## SHAPE-SHIFTING ALIEN

### VITAL STATS

**LIKES:** Cookies
**DISLIKES:** Eating meat
**FRIENDS:** Superman, Supergirl
**FOES:** Brainiac
**SKILLS:** Able to change his shape
**GEAR:** High-collared cape

**SET NAME:** Brainiac Attack
**SET NUMBER:** 76040
**YEAR:** 2015

Single-sided green head

Exclusive blue collar for this shape-shifter from Mars

Body printing on front and back based on the Martian Manhunter's classic costume

### ALTERNATE ALIEN

An earlier version of the Martian Manhunter minifigure was given away on LEGO.com in March 2014. This one had a costume based on the 2011 comic books, plus a simplified blue cape.

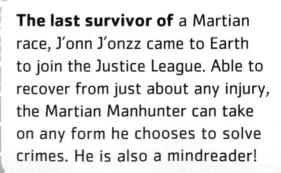

**The last survivor of** a Martian race, J'onn J'onzz came to Earth to join the Justice League. Able to recover from just about any injury, the Martian Manhunter can take on any form he chooses to solve crimes. He is also a mindreader!

# BRAINIAC
## LIVING COMPUTER

Purple wiring
printed on both
sides of minifigure

Computer
connections

Lime green
hands

### DID YOU KNOW?
Brainiac even turned
Supergirl's dad into a
cyborg, for the crime
of being a native
of Kandor City.

### KANDOR CAPER
Brainiac has clashed with
Superman on numerous
occasions, ever since the Man
of Steel discovered that the
alien android had shrunk the
Kryptonian city of Kandor.

**An alien supercomputer** from the
planet Colu, Brainiac believes that
knowledge is power. In order to
understand other races he steals
entire cities, shrinking them to fit
into jars—usually without asking
the inhabitants first.

# SKULL SHIP
## A HEAD FOR HEIGHTS

Hyperspace engines

Scary skull face

Laser cannon docks here

Terrifying tentacles!

## DOME ALONE

The transparent green dome of Brainiac's Skull Ship is not found in any other LEGO set, though a trans-clear version is used in two LEGO® Space Alien Conquest sets from 2011: UFO Abduction (set 7052) and Alien Mothership (set 7065).

Twin laser cannons

**Alien Super Villain** Brainiac controls his scary Skull Ship with the power of his mind. He can cause chaos with its two laser cannons and six twisty tentacles, and gets a 360-degree view of the action from its grisly green protective dome.

# BATZARRO

## THE WORLD'S WORST DETECTIVE

### DID YOU KNOW?
One of Batzarro's ambitions is to meet his number one hero—the Joker!

Double-sided head showing Batzarro snarling

Upside down bat-symbol and Utility Belt

Cape in tatters

### SWITCHING SIDES
Batzarro is growling on one side of his head. He may look scary, but in the end he teams up with the real Batman and the Justice League to defeat Darkseid.

**Created by Bizarro** using his LexCorp duplicator ray, Batzarro is a weird mixed-up version of the Dark Knight Detective and a member of the Bizarro League. While Batman is super-smart, Batzarro is, well, not.

# DEATHSTROKE
## MERCENARY THIEF

## VITAL STATS
....................

**LIKES:** Diamonds
**DISLIKES:** Being chased
**FRIENDS:** None
**FOES:** Batman, Robin
**SKILLS:** Piloting his jetboat
**GEAR:** Sword, gun

**SET NAME:** Batboat
Harbor Pursuit
**SET NUMBER:** 76034
**YEAR:** 2015

Two-color orange and black mask

Spare ammo ready for any mission

Two-tone legs

## MASKED MAN
The reverse of Deathstroke's mask features his trademark long headband that the mercenary sometimes wears in the comic books. His bandolier can be seen wrapping around the back of the minifigure.

**Before turning to crime,** Slade Wilson was a marine who was transformed into a soldier by the U.S. military. Tackling weapon-expert Deathstroke is always dangerous, especially when he's on the run from his latest diamond heist.

# ROBIN
## TEENAGE WONDER

## VITAL STATS

**LIKES:** Acting alone
**DISLIKES:** Not being the captain of the ship
**FRIENDS:** Batman
**FOES:** Deathstroke
**SKILLS:** Piloting hover boats
**GEAR:** Cape

**SET NAME:** Batboat Harbor Pursuit
**SET NUMBER:** 76034
**YEAR:** 2015

### DID YOU KNOW?
This minifigure reuses the Robin headpiece from Batman: The Joker Steam Roller (set 76013).

Longer hair

New body armor is more hi-tech

### RADAR ROBIN
There was nowhere to hide for Deathstroke as Batman and Robin took to the Batboat. Robin skillfully used the Bat-radar to track down the menacing mercenary.

**Dick Grayson may be** moving on to fight crime as Nightwing, but he still reappears as Robin every now and again. He can't wait for Batman to let him pilot the Batboat for himself and wears this darker suit in a fight against Deathstroke.

# BATBOAT
## BATMAN'S CATAMARAN

Radar tower lies flat at high speeds

Empty missile launcher

Levers release hovercraft from main section

## TOWER OF POWER

The tall radar tower lifts up to reveal a bank of high-tech control screens where Robin can track enemy vessels. But beware—there's a trapdoor hidden underneath!

Each cockpit has its own controls

Front blasters detach with cockpits

**Batman and Robin** are full-steam ahead in this double-hulled Batboat! Its cockpits can split off to become two hovercraft armed with blasters. The remaining control center runs on autopilot with a retractable radar tower defended by missiles.

# BATMOBILE
## HEROIC HOT ROD

### VITAL STATS

**OWNER:** Batman
**USED FOR:** Rescue missions
**GEAR:** Front and back missiles

**SET NAME:** Jokerland
**SET NUMBER:** 76035
**YEAR:** 2015

Jet turbine

Rear weaponry

Detachable cockpit canopy

Turbocharger

## DOUBLE DEFENSE

The Batmobile is armed from end to end, with two spring-loaded missiles hidden in the front turbine, and two stud shooters beneath the wings at the back.

**This Batmobile** is one huge jet engine, with a big round turbine drawing in air at the front, and a turbocharger adding extra power at the back. The roof lifts right off so Batman can leap into action at top speed, too!

# STARFIRE
## ALIEN PRINCESS

**VITAL STATS**

**LIKES:** Fun
**DISLIKES:** Misery
**FRIENDS:** Robin, Beast Boy, Batman
**FOES:** Poison Ivy, Harley Quinn, the Joker, the Penguin
**SKILLS:** Flight
**GEAR:** Starbolt energy, handcuffs, lock

**SET NAME:** Jokerland
**SET NUMBER:** 76035
**YEAR:** 2015

Long flowing purple hair

Double-sided head shows an anxious expression

Starbolt energy blasts made from green LEGO plate pieces

## STAR BRIGHT

When the Joker took over the Gotham City Funfair, Starfire and the Teen Titans flew to Batman's aid. Plants usually like light, but Poison Ivy wasn't so keen on Starfire's starbolts!

**The daughter of the** Tamaran king and queen, Princess Koriand'r absorbs solar energy through her skin and converts it to the power she needs to fly and blast emerald energy bolts from her hands. Now, she fights alongside Robin in the Teen Titans.

# BEAST BOY
## THE WILDEST KID ON THE PLANET

Grinning face

Beast Boy's pointed ears are molded to his hairpiece.

Distinctive purple outfit

Dark green hands

## BEAST VS. BIRD

A real prankster, Beast Boy loves to play practical jokes on his teammates. However, as his alternate face shows, he wasn't so happy to find himself tricked and trapped in a duck prison by the Penguin.

**Garfield Logan is** a bit of every animal. The Teen Titan can transform himself into any bird or beast, thanks to a special serum that saved him from a toxic animal bite as a child. Unfortunately it left him with green colored skin in return!

# HARLEY QUINN
## HUMOROUS HIGH ROLLER

## VITAL STATS

**LIKES:** Silly stunts
**DISLIKES:** Being serious
**FRIENDS:** The Joker, Poison Ivy, the Penguin
**FOES:** Robin, Batman, Starfire, Beast Boy
**SKILLS:** Stunt riding
**GEAR:** Giant hammer, stunt motorcycle

**SET NAME:** Jokerland
**SET NUMBER:** 76035
**YEAR:** 2015

This is the first Harley minifigure not to feature her eye mask.

New body printing complete with bells around Harley's neck

### DID YOU KNOW?
This outfit was based on a new costume first introduced to the comics in 2014.

### HIGH-WIRE HAVOC
Harley's "Wheels of Fire" motorcycle can be sent rolling down its slope with a flick of a sign. Harley is enjoying the ride a lot more than the upside-down Robin stuck underneath!

Printing continues on the side of Harley's legs

Red and black gloves

**In her new acrobat suit,** the Clown Princess of Crime doesn't wear her usual mask, opting for dark make-up around her eyes. She still loves a laugh though, and uses her over-sized weapon to hammer home any punch line.

## VITAL STATS

**LIKES:** Leading his team
**DISLIKES:** Getting caught
**FRIENDS:** Starfire, Beast Boy, Batman
**FOES:** Harley Quinn, the Joker, the Penguin, Poison Ivy
**SKILLS:** Circus tricks, balance
**GEAR:** Staff, handcuffs, lock

**SET NAME:** Jokerland
**SET NUMBER:** 76035
**YEAR:** 2015

Spiky hair

Double-sided head showing shocked expression

New stretchy cape

### THE FIRST ROBIN

Based on his Teen Titans costume, this minifigure shows Robin with his original insignia and short sleeved arms. A turn of his head shows a determined expression too.

**Dick Grayson helped** found the Teen Titans, and was certainly pleased to see his teammates when he found himself locked up by Harley Quinn in the Joker's twisted fun-scare. Of course, he claimed getting caught was all part of the plan!

**JOKERLAND**

In potentially the most colorful LEGO DC Comics Super Heroes set to date: Jokerland (set 76035), the Joker unleashes a diabolical funfair-themed scheme to trap Batman. Every villain has a ride themed to them.

# ARSENAL

## THE RED ARROW

### VITAL STATS
......................

**LIKES:** Fighting crime
**DISLIKES:** Being called Speedy
**FRIENDS:** Green Arrow
**FOES:** Deathstroke
**SKILLS:** Archery
**GEAR:** Longbow

**SET NAME:** Arsenal San Diego Comic-Con Exclusive
**SET NUMBER:** SDCC2015
**YEARS:** 2015

Red hood based on the costume from the Arrow TV show

Black version of Green Arrow's longbow

Leather straps printed on chest

### READY TO FIRE
The back of the exclusive minifigure shows a quiver of arrows ready to fire. Arsenal also has a double-sided head complete with a snarling face on the reverse.

**When Arrow took** martial art expert Roy Harper under his wing he tried to call his new sidekick Speedy. Harper hated the name, christening himself Arsenal instead. The young archer is almost as good a shot as his green-hooded mentor.

# TRICKSTER
## PRANKS A LOT!

## VITAL STATS

**LIKES:** Tricking people
**DISLIKES:** Being tricked
**FRIENDS:** Captain Cold
**FOES:** The Flash
**SKILLS:** Telling jokes
**GEAR:** Anti-gravity boots

**SET NAMES:** LEGO *DC Comics Super Heroes Justice League: Attack of the Legion of Doom!* DVD movie
**YEARS:** 2015

Two-color arms suggest T-shirt sleeves

No other LEGO minifigure has hair this color

Belt and braces lined with gadget pouches

### REAR-AXEL

The Trickster's belt and braces printing continues on his back, adding more pouches in which he can store twisted trick items such as itching powder and exploding rubber chickens!

Checkered pattern continues on side of legs

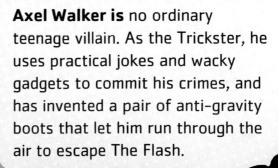

**Axel Walker is** no ordinary teenage villain. As the Trickster, he uses practical jokes and wacky gadgets to commit his crimes, and has invented a pair of anti-gravity boots that let him run through the air to escape The Flash.

# DEADSHOT
## MASKED MARKSMAN

DEADSHOT

## VITAL STATS

**LIKES:** Moving targets
**DISLIKES:** Feeling aimless
**FRIENDS:** Harley Quinn
**FOES:** Batman
**SKILLS:** Expert aim
**GEAR:** Built-in guns and targeting tech

**SET NAMES:** Batman: Gotham City Cycle Chase
**SET NUMBERS:** 76053
**YEARS:** 2016

Gun sight built into mask

Armored suit can withstand explosions

Wrist-mounted guns on arm

### GUN FOR HIGH-UP HIRE

Deadshot is really skyrocketing with this jetpack and bazooka combo! The giant weapon is made from eight pieces and can fire studs on Batman and his friends below.

**This sharpshooter** likes to boast that he never misses a target. He wears a metal mask with a special eyepiece to help him take aim, and has weapons built in to the arms of his suit. Sometimes he fights crime, but he prefers to battle Batman!

# HARLEY QUINN
## TRICOLOR TRICKSTER

## VITAL STATS
...................................

**LIKES:** Hair dye
**DISLIKES:** Being serious
**FRIENDS:** Deadshot
**FOES:** Batman
**SKILLS:** Gymnastics
**GEAR:** Giant hammer

**SET NAMES:** Batman: Gotham City Cycle Chase
**SET NUMBERS:** 76053
**YEARS:** 2016

Unique red and blue hairpiece

Harley's bare arms are as white as her face!

Brutal belt of bullets

Corset design continues on back

### HARLEY GRIM

Harley's double-sided head turns to reveal an angry glare and gritted teeth. It's the face that the chaos-loving criminal wears when she brings out her big hammer!

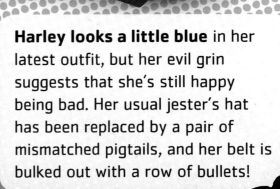

**Harley looks a little blue** in her latest outfit, but her evil grin suggests that she's still happy being bad. Her usual jester's hat has been replaced by a pair of mismatched pigtails, and her belt is bulked out with a row of bullets!

## DRIVETIME HITS

### VITAL STATS

**OWNER:** Harley Quinn
**USED FOR:** Going flat out
**GEAR:** Hammer attachment

**SET NAMES:** Batman:
Gotham City Cycle Chase
**SET NUMBERS:** 76053
**YEARS:** 2016

Hammer has
"POW!" written
on one end.

One of four exhausts
needed to power
enormous engine

Bigger wheel
at front

Laser cannons flank
front wheel

### WHACK ATTACK

Harley's hammer can be fixed on
to the bike in two different
ways, so that it can swing from
side to side, or back and forth.
It has a diamond design that is
similar to a harlequin's suit.

**Harley likes** to smash speed
records on her motorcycle. In fact,
she likes to smash everything! Her
massive mallet fits on to the side
of the bike and is ready to whack
anyone overtaking in the next lane.
Batman had better watch out!

# BAT-CYCLE
## LONGER, WIDER, STRONGER

### VITAL STATS
........................

**OWNER:** Batman
**USED FOR:** Narrow escapes
**GEAR:** Grapple, shooters

**SET NAMES:** Batman: Gotham City Cycle Chase
**SET NUMBERS:** 76053
**YEARS:** 2016

Afterburner glows with heat

Silver Batarang stored at the back

Bat-symbol on fuel tank

### ARMED ARMS
Backward-facing shooters on both sides of the rear wheel can flip round and fire to the front or sides. The right-hand arm also has a grapple gun, and the left holds a Batarang.

Laser cannons in front lights

**Batman's motorcycle** has wheels as wide as he is! The Caped Crusader keeps a low profile between the monster-truck tires and dual shooters can target enemies tearing away in front of the bike or giving chase behind it.

169

# LEX LUTHOR
## *LEXCORP LEADER*

Unusually, this Lex minifigure has locks!

## VITAL STATS
..........................

**LIKES:** Having hair, helicopters
**DISLIKES:** Super Hero team-ups
**FRIENDS:** Henchmen
**FOES:** Superman, Wonder Woman, Batman
**SKILLS:** Computer coding
**GEAR:** Double-barreled handgun

**SET NAMES:** Heroes of Justice: Sky-High Battle
**SET NUMBERS:** 76046
**YEARS:** 2016

Smart-casual sand-colored clothes of a tech company boss.

## HAIR RAISER
This LexCorp helicopter has eight Kryptonite missiles to launch against Superman—but Lex can't stop Wonder Woman coming to rescue Lois.

**Lex luxuriates** in long hair and a leisure suit for his latest, laid-back look. There's nothing relaxed about his grimace and gun however, which he uses to menace Lois Lane. Perhaps he knows he's still bald under that LEGO hair piece!

## GRIZZLED GUARD

### VITAL STATS

**LIKES:** LexCorp staff benefits
**DISLIKES:** Not getting to drive the forklift truck
**FRIENDS:** Other henchmen
**FOES:** Batman, Superman
**SKILLS:** Guarding things
**GEAR:** Bazooka

**SET NAMES:** Kryptonite Interception
**SET NUMBERS:** 76045
**YEARS:** 2016

LexCorp ID badge

Black gloves for doing dirty work

Stud-shooting bazooka rifle

### BADDIE BUDDY

The henchman's pal wears the same uniform and a similar scowl, but is clean-shaven. Together they guard a secret stash of LexCorp Kryptonite.

LEXCORP

**A henchman** needs an impressive resumé to work at LexCorp, and this bearded baddie lists guard duty and bazooka skills among his many talents. In return for loyalty to Lex, he gets a smart green uniform and access to hi-tech weapons.

# ARMORED BATMAN
## GLOWERS IN THE DARK

## VITAL STATS

**LIKES:** Saving the world
**DISLIKES:** Mysterious aliens
**FRIENDS:** Alfred
**FOES:** Superman
**SKILLS:** Armored combat
**GEAR:** Bazooka, grapple,
Batarang

**SET NAMES:** Clash of
the Heroes
**SET NUMBERS:** 76044
**YEARS:** 2016

Glow-in-the-
dark eyes

Chunky
armor
covers
torso

Silver Batarang
fixes on back

## BAZOOKA BUILD

Batman's three-in-one weapon
can be built as a stud-shooting
bazooka with two handles, or as
a smaller stud-shooter and a
separate grapple launcher for
Batman to hold in each hand.

**Sometimes,** even Super Heroes
squabble—and when Batman takes
on Superman in a rooftop duel, he'll
need his most impressive armor!
This combat suit has grips to store
equipment and protective plating.

# SUPERMAN
## SUITED AND REBOOTED

### VITAL STATS

**LIKES:** Saving the world
**DISLIKES:** Kryptonite missiles
**FRIENDS:** Lois Lane
**FOES:** Lex Luthor
**SKILLS:** Heat vision, X-ray vision
**GEAR:** Heat vision

**SET NAMES:** Heroes of Justice: Sky-High Battle
**SET NUMBERS:** 76046
**YEARS:** 2016

All versions of Superman have a chiseled jaw, but only this one wears this broad grin.

New LEGO hair piece

Red cape is the only element shared with other Superman minifigures.

Red boots printed on legs

### RED-EYE

Superman sports angry red eyes in Clash of the Heroes (set 76044). Maybe it's his heat vision, or perhaps he's cross that he's lost his bright red boots!

**Batman and Superman** must save Lois from the clutches of Lex Luthor in his LexCorp helicopter. Superman has a whole new outfit with bright red boots, a heroic new hairstyle, and alternate expressions on his double-sided face.

# BATWING
## FLYING ALL THROUGH THE NIGHT

### VITAL STATS

**OWNER:** Batman
**USED FOR:** Chasing Lex Luthor
**GEAR:** Rapid-fire shooter

**SET NAMES:** Heroes of Justice: Sky-High Battle
**SET NUMBERS:** 76046
**YEARS:** 2016

Cockpit opens in two sections

### DID YOU KNOW?
The Batwing's rotating cannon has six rapid-fire launchers. Lex Luthor, in his helicopter, needs to watch out!

Small silver bat-symbol on cannon

### WINGING IT

In flight, the Batwing gains lift by extending its wings in a "V" formation. In landing mode, its wings retract and its fins fold up to create a smaller and squarer silhouette.

Wings fully extended for flight mode

**When Superman** is on the scene, Batman needs wings to keep up with the action! The Caped Crusader jumps into this stealth flyer to join the Last Son of Krypton in pursuit of Lex Luthor.

## FIGHTING FOR JUSTICE

### VITAL STATS

**LIKES:** Animals
**DISLIKES:** War
**FRIENDS:** Superman
**FOES:** Lex Luthor
**SKILLS:** Amazonian martial arts
**GEAR:** Sword and shield

**SET NAMES:** Heroes of Justice: Sky-High Battle
**SET NUMBERS:** 76046
**YEARS:** 2016

Hair piece is new for 2016.

### DID YOU KNOW?

All earlier minifigure versions of Wonder Woman have her royal headband molded as part of the hair piece.

Gold chestplate is shaped like an eagle.

Bulletproof bracelets on both arms

### FACE TO FACE

Wonder Woman's head turns to reveal determined eyes and gritted teeth as she heads into battle. She is armed with her trusty sword and a shield with an eagle motif.

**Wonder Woman** uses lightning-fast reflexes to deflect bullets with her armor bracelets, and is ready for whatever Lex Luthor can throw at her. She knows that their battle will mean the difference between war and the dawn of justice!

# LOIS LANE
## STAR OF THE PLANET

### VITAL STATS
..........................

**LIKES:** Exclusives
**DISLIKES:** Cover-ups
**FRIENDS:** Superman
**FOES:** Lex Luthor
**SKILLS:** Getting to the truth
**GEAR:** Camera

**SET NAMES:** Heroes of
Justice: Sky-High Battle
**SET NUMBERS:** 76046
**YEARS:** 2016

Serious face
can be swapped
for scared look

Camera for capturing
breaking news

### A NOSE FOR NEWS
Lois loves to investigate and
often gets into danger following
her reporter's instincts. When
she starts to ask questions
about Lex Luthor, she ends up
hanging from his helicopter!

Smart suit for
doing interviews

**Ace news reporter** Lois Lane
knows Superman's secret, but he
trusts her not to print it in the *Daily
Planet*! With a camera in her hand
and a big story in her sights, there's
nowhere Lois won't go to find the
facts for tomorrow's headlines.

# BATMOBILE
## CARRIAGE OF JUSTICE

### VITAL STATS

**OWNER:** Batman
**USED FOR:** Getting around Gotham City
**GEAR:** Front and side cannons

**SET NAMES:** Kryptonite Interception
**SET NUMBERS:** 76045
**YEARS:** 2016

Cockpit opens in two sections

Armored plates protect rear wheels

Stud shooters at front

Recessed front lights

### FORK IN THE ROAD
A forklift truck might seem like no match for the Batmobile, but this LexCorp model is armed with flick missiles and driven by a henchman with a stud-shooting bazooka!

**Ideal for a trip** to Metropolis, this Batmobile is heavily armed and armored against superpowered attack. Silver details include side vents and a shield-like bat-symbol on the hood, plus shiny shooters to bring a touch of bling to any battle!

# BATMAN
## BACK WITH A "BAM!"

### VITAL STATS

**LIKES:** Law-abiding citizens
**DISLIKES:** Dastardly traps
**FRIENDS:** Robin, Alfred
**FOES:** Catwoman, the Joker, the Penguin, the Riddler
**SKILLS:** Science, math, grammar
**GEAR:** Batarang

**SET NAMES:** *Batman* Classic TV Series—Batcave
**SET NUMBERS:** 76052
**YEARS:** 2016

Physique shows through tight suit

Cowl with printed frown

Trusty Batarang

### TRUE OR FALSE?

Batman has all sorts of high-tech equipment in his Batcave laboratory, including a huge atomic reactor, radar screens, and a lie detector with green and red lights on top.

**Batman is a brilliant inventor** and his unique Utility Belt is full of gadgets for every occasion. He has even invented a dance called the "Batusi." It helps him keep in shape for his never-ending battle against the rogues of Gotham City!

# BRUCE WAYNE

## THE MAN BEHIND THE MASK

Neat, no-nonsense hair

Stylish cravat in open shirt

Wayne family crest on blazer

### DID YOU KNOW?
The classic *Batman* TV series ran for three seasons between 1966 and 1968, with a total of 120 episodes!

### RED ALERT
As well as being filled with all his sporting trophies, Bruce's study is also home to a bright red telephone. This gives the Gotham City police a direct line to Batman and Robin.

**The billionaire owner** of Wayne Manor is accomplished at riding horseback, fishing, climbing, and marbles. He gives money to charity and cares for his young ward, Dick Grayson. On top of that, he has a sharp suit—and he's also Batman!

# ALFRED
## FAITHFUL FRIEND

White handkerchief in breast pocket

Batphone for receiving calls from Commissioner Gordon

### YOU RANG, SIR?
Alfred's daily duties include answering the Batphone. He summons Batman if he is at home, and takes messages from Commissioner Gordon if the Caped Crusader is out.

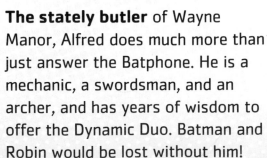

**The stately butler** of Wayne Manor, Alfred does much more than just answer the Batphone. He is a mechanic, a swordsman, and an archer, and has years of wisdom to offer the Dynamic Duo. Batman and Robin would be lost without him!

# DICK GRAYSON
## WARD OF WAYNE MANOR

Dick models his neat hair after Bruce Wayne's

Sensible red sweater over white shirt

Smart blue pants

### BATCAVE OR BUST

When duty calls, Dick flips up the bust of Shakespeare on Bruce's desk to reveal a hidden button. Pressing it opens up a secret entrance to the Batcave!

**Being Dick Grayson** sure is tough! His legal guardian, Bruce Wayne, makes him study hard when he'd rather be working out in the gym. But when Bruce explains it's all part of being a Boy Wonder, Dick reckons life is not so bad after all.

# THE JOKER
## CACKLING PRINCE OF CRIME

### VITAL STATS

**LIKES:** Laughing
**DISLIKES:** Being laughed at
**FRIENDS:** Catwoman, the Penguin, the Riddler
**FOES:** Batman and Robin
**SKILLS:** Magic tricks and making gadgets
**GEAR:** Laboratory flask

**SET NAMES:** *Batman* Classic TV Series—Batcave
**SET NUMBERS:** 76052
**YEARS:** 2016

Greasepaint covers mustache

Three-piece suit packed with pranks

Beaker full of potent chemicals

### LAB GRAB

When the Joker gets his hands on Batman's lab, who knows what chemical concoctions he will cook up! Going by the grin on his reversible head, it might be a batch of laughing gas.

**With his grotesque grin,** green hair, and bright pink suit, the Joker is never going to make it as a sneak thief! Instead he likes to live large as he launches plots to steal paintings, build a flying saucer, and beat Batman at a surfing contest.

# CATWOMAN
## PURRING PLUNDERER

# CATWOMAN

## VITAL STATS

**LIKES:** Long stretches
**DISLIKES:** Long stretches in jail
**FRIENDS:** The Joker, the Penguin, the Riddler
**FOES:** Batman and Robin
**SKILLS:** Cat burglary
**GEAR:** Gas-filled whip

**SET NAMES:** *Batman* Classic TV Series—Batcave
**SET NUMBERS:** 76052
**YEARS:** 2016

Cat ears attached to hairband

Catty look can be swapped for a merrier, masked face

Gold medallion worn over catsuit

### THE CAT CAME BACK
Catwoman knows all about Wayne Manor after posing as Dick Grayson's dance teacher. She's not scared of falling as she scales its walls, because a cat will always land on its feet!

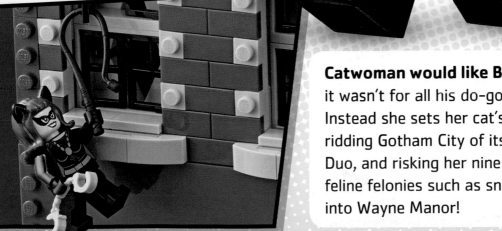

**Catwoman would like Batman** if it wasn't for all his do-gooding! Instead she sets her cat's eyes on ridding Gotham City of its Dynamic Duo, and risking her nine lives on feline felonies such as sneaking into Wayne Manor!

# THE RIDDLER
## AN ENIGMA

## VITAL STATS

**LIKES:** Quizzes and conundrums
**DISLIKES:** Easy answers
**FRIENDS:** Catwoman, the Joker, the Penguin
**FOES:** Batman and Robin
**SKILLS:** Chemistry, cryptography
**GEAR:** Dynamite

**SET NAMES:** *Batman* Classic TV Series—Batcave
**SET NUMBERS:** 76052
**YEARS:** 2016

Head rotates to reveal gleeful grin

Dynamite to destroy the Batcave!

Silk cummerbund matches gloves and mask

## RIDDLE ME THIS...

What three letters make the sound of an explosion? TNT! The Riddler is out to blow the roof off Wayne Manor.

**When does a question mark** mean danger? When it's printed on the Riddler's outfit! This puzzling pest always leaves clues to his quizzical crimes, luring Batman and Robin into baffling booby traps that seem to have no answer.

# ROBIN
## BRIGHT AND BREEZY

### VITAL STATS
........................

**LIKES:** Riding in the Batmobile
**DISLIKES:** Not getting to drive the Batmobile
**FRIENDS:** Batman, Alfred
**FOES:** Catwoman, the Joker, the Penguin, the Riddler
**SKILLS:** Honesty, courage
**GEAR:** Handcuffs

**SET NAMES:** *Batman* Classic TV Series—Batcave
**SET NUMBERS:** 76052
**YEARS:** 2016

Reverse of head shows alarmed face

Tunic laces up at front

Flesh-colored tights protect legs

### TO THE BATPOLES!
Quick-change Batpoles in the Batcave allow Bruce Wayne and Dick Grayson to become Batman and Robin at the flick of a switch on their way down to the Batmobile.

**This colorful sidekick** needs an equally colorful oufit. Clad in a smart red tunic and very short green shorts, Robin is ready to save the day in style. That's what makes him Batman's best chum and a vital part of the Dynamic Duo!

# BATMOBILE
## WELL-EQUIPPED WHEELS

## VITAL STATS

**OWNER:** Batman
**USED FOR:** Foiling diabolical schemes
**GEAR:** Shooters, grapples

**SET NAMES:** *Batman* Classic TV Series—Batcave
**SET NUMBERS:** 76052
**YEARS:** 2016

Batphone hidden between seats

Dual exhaust pipes

### GRAPPLES AND PAIRS
The trunk of the Batmobile opens to reveal enough room for two grappling hooks and ropes for scaling the sides of buildings, three Batarangs, and a pair of handcuffs.

Bazookas for blasting through walls

**Pow! Blasting out** from the Batcave beneath stately Wayne Manor, this gadget-packed Batmobile is the coolest car of the 1960s. Gotham City was pretty different back then, but the Dynamic Duo never go out of fashion!

# BATCOPTER
## EARLY WHIRLYBIRD

Wings cast
a shadow to
scare crooks.

Domed cockpit for
an all-round view.

## MADE FOR TWO

The Boy Wonder takes another
seat in the sidecar of this
two-person Batcycle. It has
space for a handy spare tire and
is also part of the *Batman*
Classic TV Series Batcave set.

Missile in
flight

**Robin takes the controls** of this
classic 'copter, which dates from the
same time and communicates on the
same channel as the Batmobile on
p.113. It has wings to aid its flight
and shark-repelling missiles for
missions at sea!

# THE PENGUIN
## ANTARCTIC ADVERSARY

## VITAL STATS
..........................

**LIKES:** Fish and all birds
except robins
**DISLIKES:** Mammals,
especially bats
**FRIENDS:** Catwoman,
the Joker, the Riddler
**FOES:** Batman and Robin
**SKILLS:** Squawking, scheming
**GEAR:** Umbrella

**SET NAMES:** *Batman* Classic
TV Series—Batcave
**SET NUMBERS:** 76052
**YEARS:** 2016

The Penguin thinks
that a top hat makes
him look taller.

The Penguin's belly
is too big for his
tight jacket!

White gloves
cover hands

### HIGH AND DRY

When the Penguin sticks his
beak into the Batcave, he floats
in on his trademark umbrella,
which can also shoot knockout
gas, cut glass, self-destruct—
and even keep the rain off!

**Foes don't come** fishier than this
feather-ruffling ruffian! Waddling
his way through the murky waters
of Gotham City's underworld, this
version of the Penguin is sporting
a new lilac-colored top hat
and bow tie!

# PIRATE BATMAN

## BOOK BUCCANEER

### VITAL STATS

**LIKES:** Buried treasure
**DISLIKES:** Walking the plank
**FRIENDS:** The sea
**FOES:** Brainiac
**SKILLS:** Swashbuckling
**GEAR:** Flail, cutlass

**SET NAMES:** DK's LEGO *DC Comics Character Encyclopedia*
**YEARS:** 2016

**DID YOU KNOW?**
This exclusive minifigure is only available with the trade edition of DK's LEGO *DC Comics Super Heroes Character Encyclopedia*.

No other Batman minifigure wears this chinless cowl in blue

Spiked flail for self-defense

Utility Belt worn across chest

### BACK THROUGH TIME

Pirate Batman is the only LEGO version so far to feature a bat-symbol on the back of his torso (though it is partly hidden by his piratical Utility Belt).

Curved sword called a cutlass

**Shiver me timbers** – Batman's a buccaneer! Thrown back in time by Brainiac's Time Ray, this Dark Knight dresses as a pirate to fit in with the seafarers he finds himself amongst. He must rescue Green Lantern before returning to the present day!

**NEW BATCAVE**
March 2016 saw the release of a very special LEGO Batcave (set 76052)—in honor of the 1960s *Batman* TV series.

# CATWOMAN
## KITTEN-SIZED CRIMINAL

MIGHTY MICROS

**VITAL STATS**

**LIKES:** Diamonds
**DISLIKES:** Dogs
**FRIENDS:** None
**FOES:** Mighty Micros: Batman
**SKILLS:** Cat burglary
**GEAR:** Milk carton

**SET NAME:** Mighty Micros: Batman vs. Catwoman
**SET NUMBER:** 76061
**YEAR:** 2016

Cute cat mask disguises a criminal mastermind

Purr-ple lipstick

Belt with cat's-head clasp

Kitten heels

## KITTY CAR
Catwoman is the cat who got the cream in her Mighty Micros car. It has cat's eyes and ears between the headlights, and between the taillights—a tail!

**This cat always** lands on her feet, even though her legs don't bend! Clad in a panther-black catsuit, the feline felon can slip into even the smallest nook or cranny, pilfering everything from priceless jewels to a plate of milk!

# MIGHTY MICRO BATMAN

## DIMINUTIVE DARK KNIGHT

Determined jaw under chinless cowl

Utility Belt holds up mini pants

Cape flows down to the ground

Scaled-up bat-symbol fits with wackier Mighty Micros universe.

## VITAL STATS

**LIKES:** Microscopes
**DISLIKES:** Micromanagement
**FRIENDS:** Mighty Micros: Robin
**FOES:** Mighty Micros: Catwoman
**SKILLS:** Making short work of villains
**GEAR:** Batarang

**SET NAMES:** Mighty Micros: Batman vs. Catwoman
**SET NUMBERS:** 76061
**YEARS:** 2016

## CARTON CAPERS

Batman can snatch stolen milk from Catwoman's claws in his Mighty Micros Batmobile. With a super-speedy afterburner, it's just the thing for a dairy derby!

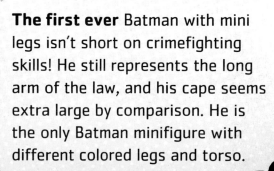

**The first ever** Batman with mini legs isn't short on crimefighting skills! He still represents the long arm of the law, and his cape seems extra large by comparison. He is the only Batman minifigure with different colored legs and torso.

## SMALL WONDER

### VITAL STATS

**LIKES:** Scaling new heights
**DISLIKES:** Being grounded
**FRIENDS:** Mighty Micros: Batman
**FOES:** Mighty Micros: Bane
**SKILLS:** Climbing, acrobatics
**GEAR:** Grapple gun

**SET NAMES:** Mighty Micros: Bane vs. Robin
**SET NUMBERS:** 76062
**YEARS:** 2016

Same neat hair as red-suited Robin (p.45)

Mask doesn't hide Robin's happy eyes!

Shorter cape than most Robin minifigures

Non-posable legs

### RELIANT ROBIN

Robin can rely on his Mighty Micros car to get him around on the ground, but he also carries a grapple gun, in case there are any walls to climb!

**There's nothing** at all micro about the smile on this Robin's face! The larger-than-life character couldn't be happier to have his own car for the first time, and he's going to use it to stop Mighty Micros: Bane from causing big trouble in Gotham City!

**MIGHTY MICROS**

## VITAL STATS

**LIKES:** Drilling tunnels, tunneling drills
**DISLIKES:** Taking his mask off
**FRIENDS:** His teddy bear
**FOES:** Mighty Micros: Robin
**SKILLS:** Plotting and planning
**GEAR:** Dynamite

**SET NAME:** Mighty Micros: Robin vs. Bane
**SET NUMBER:** 76062
**YEAR:** 2016

Mask hides the tubes that pump Bane full of Venom

No other Bane minifigure wears a top like this

Same black mini legs as Mighty Micros Batman

## JUST A LITTLE BIT

Bane's Mighty Micros drill tank has a shiny rotating drill bit at the front and flaming chimneys at the back. Bane himself lobs dynamite from the driving seat!

**The red "B"** on his chest stands for Bane, but it could also be for bad, brawny, and brutal! He might not be at his biggest here, but Bane is still one of Batman's most imposing opponents, towering over others in terms of brains and beef!

# MIGHTY MICROS: THE FLASH
## SHORT-DISTANCE RUNNER

## VITAL STATS

**LIKES:** Fast cars
**DISLIKES:** Dawdlers
**FRIENDS:** Mighty Micros
Batman, Mighty Micros: Robin
**FOES:** Mighty Micros:
Captain Cold
**SKILLS:** Quick thinking
**GEAR:** Energy drink

**SET NAME:** Mighty Micros:
The Flash vs. Captain Cold
**SET NUMBER:** 76063
**YEAR:** 2016

Wings on mask are a symbol of speed

All parts of minifigure are red—other colors are printed

Small, confident smile peeks out from mask

Lightning bolts hint at how Barry Allen became The Flash

## FLASH DRIVE

This Mighty Micros race car might not be as fast as The Flash himself, but it gives his legs a rest while he enjoys his can of Power Bolt energy drink!

**The Flash loves** to stretch his legs. In fact, he runs so fast, you can't even see his bottom half move! The micro marathon man is hot on the heels of chilly criminal Captain Cold. He reckons a bit of exercise should warm him up!

## COMPACT FREEZER

### VITAL STATS
.......................

**LIKES:** Chilling out
**DISLIKES:** Global warming
**FRIENDS:** Snowmen
**FOES:** Mighty Micros: The Flash
**SKILLS:** Making ice weapons
**GEAR:** Freeze gun, snow cone

**SET NAME:** Mighty Micros: The Flash vs. Captain Cold
**SET NUMBER:** 76063
**YEAR:** 2016

Despite his name, Captain Cold likes to wrap up warm.

Cold eyes hidden by thick goggles.

MIGHTY MICROS

### DID YOU KNOW?
Captain Cold is the leader of a criminal gang called the Rogues. Its members include the Trickster (see p.165).

### PLOWING ON
With a snow cone in one hand and his freeze gun on full blast in the other, Captain Cold uses this Mighty Micros snow plow to find his way through the ice.

Mini legs are frozen stiff!

**Look out**—there's a mini ice age coming! Ice-cool villain Captain Cold makes his own microclimate with his fearsome freeze gun and his frosty manner. He would love to fast-freeze The Flash in a big block of ice!

### What does it mean to be a LEGO® Model Designer?
I design brick-built models, which could be vehicles, such as the Batmobile or the Riddler's Dragster, but also playsets of buildings and structures within the DC Comics universe. Just recently I have also started designing LEGO® elements, too.

### Have you always been a LEGO fan?
I was always a LEGO fan—I have great memories of playing with LEGO sets and DUPLO® sets with my siblings while growing up. A personal highlight for me was the first LEGO Pirates launch in 1989. We played with that range for hours. The Black Seas Barracuda Pirate Ship (set 6285) was my personal favorite.

Black Manta's helmet (from set 76027) was created using the "2K" element molding technique.

### How did you come to work at the LEGO Group?
I never thought that I would work for the LEGO Group! However, I was always creative as a kid and went on to do a Bachelor's degree in Industrial Design in Ireland. I was designing street furniture (such as litterbins and benches) when I made the jump to LEGO toy design! I heard about a Product Design job at the LEGO Group being advertised, so I applied. I was invited to fly out to Denmark for an interview and I got it. It's been a very interesting journey!

### How do you plan out the sets alongside DC Comics?
The process varies. Sometimes we might be designing for a particular film or TV series, such as the 2016 *Batman v Superman: Dawn of Justice* movie. In that instance we receive scripts and other reference materials so we can think about what might be fun builds for children. Other times we might want a more classic feel for a set and we take our inspiration directly from the DC Comics and their world. In addition, DC Comics might want us to explore particular characters and models. It's a constant dialogue. It also depends on what story we want to tell on the LEGO set box. For example, if we want to create a sub-zero theme set, then it's natural to go straight to Mr. Freeze! In another set, Batman: Man-Bat Attack (set 76011), Batman's helicopter is not from any particular movie or cartoon but is totally something that Batman might have in his Batcave!

### How do you go about designing and building sets?

We initially brainstorm as a team and propose models, stories, and characters that will make great LEGO sets. We are then assigned to work on a set as an individual designer. This was the case with the 2015 Jokerland set (76035): we all brainstormed and built bits and pieces that might go into a themepark based set. A lot of our decisions come down to what a character's role might be within the set—something might suit one character but not another. For example, the motorcycle within Jokerland really suits Harley Quinn as she's such a daredevil. Equally, the Venus Flytrap elements really work for Poison Ivy.

### Are there any exciting new elements that you have designed recently?

We recently designed two cockpit elements, one left and one right, exclusively for the Batman v Superman Batmobile (set 76045) and Batwing (set 76046). They were directly inspired from the way the vehicles look and work in the movie.

In the case of Black Manta Deep Sea Strike (set 76027), for example, this set was not based directly on any specific comic or film. But we still designed a very distinctive helmet for Black Manta himself, trying very hard to make a design that would meet fan expectations and would be a really cool piece. To get this result we used a "2K process" where we mold two different materials together to make one element. Also, when it came to designing Batgirl and her cowl, we could possibly have used Batman's existing cowl, but we wanted to show off her flowing hair, and so we designed a new headpiece, especially for her.

John is pictured with the new Batwing model, appearing in 2016 (set 76046).

### Do you have a personal favorite LEGO DC Comics Super Heroes set?

My favorite set would probably have to be the first LEGO set I designed—Arctic Batman vs. Mr Freeze: Aquaman on Ice (set 76000)—which will always have a special space in my heart. It's a very cool thing to design a LEGO set when you have had this huge love for LEGO models from when you were a kid. Also, this was really one of the very first sets we designed that explored a different type of mission for Batman with a different style of costume. Plus it has a really fun story to go with it!

### Are there any DC Comics characters not yet in LEGO form that you would love to see?

As a kid I was a big Batman fan. And the great thing about Batman is that he has loads of really cool villains to go up against. I would love to see a LEGO Rā's al Ghūl minifigure. He has a cool story and an interesting dynamic with Batman—respecting him but wanting to defeat him at the same time!

## SENIOR GRAPHIC DESIGNER

**What is it like being a LEGO® Graphic Designer?**
Being a graphic designer encompasses designing the minifigures and all the minifigure decoration— their expressions, their torsos and legs, and also any details on the brick-built models, such as the Batman logo, or stickers and other decorations.

Adam shows off the Batman minifigure from the 2016 sets, with his new armor and boots.

**How did you come to work at the LEGO Group?**
I happened to be displaying some work at an exhibition in London and the LEGO Group were looking for new graduates so I applied. Since I joined I have mostly worked in the Super Heroes team, but also on other projects such as THE LEGO® MOVIE™, where I really enjoyed designing the "Where Are My Pants" minifigure.

**How do you decide which minifigures to make?**
There's lots of talk within the design team and with DC Comics about any specific characters that we would want to make and what would be cool. We also bring into the discussion what version of the characters we would like to see—for example, Batman has so many suits: do we want to see him in space with a space suit or does he need an underwater suit for the story we want to tell within the set as a whole?

**What's new for LEGO DC Comics Super Heroes?**
Our first LEGO DC Comics Super Heroes bigfigs—Darkseid and Gorilla Grodd—were a fun challenge to design as while they are scaled up, they still need to look as cool as a minifigure. For example, Darkseid maintains his minifigure-style eyes. We also got to bring a really fun sense of humor into the Gorilla Grodd set (76026). I enjoyed creating the screaming face for the scared Truck Driver!

**Do you have a favorite LEGO DC Comics Super Heroes set?**
If I had to choose just one then I'd say Green Lantern vs. Sinestro (set 76025). It's such a colorful set, with a bright pink and yellow Sinestro, and it features a Green Lantern minifigure in a set for the first time. Also, the new Batman from this set inspired the Batman from the latest video game. It was a challenge to create those space wings for Batman, with two options for open and closed.

**Are there any DC Comics characters not yet in LEGO form that you would love to see?**
One minifigure that I really wanted to see before I ever came to work for LEGO DC Comics Super Heroes was Batman of Zur-En-Arrh (San Diego Comic-Con 2014). I love it because we never normally get to see Batman in such bright, wacky colors.

**What's next for LEGO DC Comics Super Heroes?**
The Batmobile for the new *Batman v Superman: Dawn of Justice* movie is looking really cool. We're all really excited to see what DC Comics will bring to the table.

**How do you decide which exclusives to make?**
When we talk about characters for books and other exclusive releases we think it has to be really cool—and something that perhaps wouldn't appear in a set. Batman has so many variants, so we work with DC Comics to figure out what we would like to see. For this book we chose Pirate Batman, and used the comics as points of reference.

Graphic Designer Daniel McKenna designs minifigures, such as Pirate Batman.

**Daniel McKenna helped to design DK's exclusive, Pirate Batman, and talked to us about the process:**
We did a number of designs to begin with, including a Caveman Batman and a Pirate Batman. I loved the zany quirky comedy of the pirate costume contrasted with the seriousness of Batman. We went through several versions to ensure that he remained recognizably and iconically Batman but with fun, piratical elements.

# SET GALLERY

**A treat for all** LEGO® fans, here are all the LEGO DC Comics Super Heroes sets produced so far. How many have you collected? Do you have a favorite? With some exciting new sets releasing in 2016 and beyond, it's time to get them all!

## 2006

**7779**
**THE BATMAN DRAGSTER:**
**CATWOMAN PURSUIT**

**7780**
**THE BATBOAT: HUNT FOR**
**KILLER CROC**

**7781**
**THE BATMOBILE:**
**TWO-FACE'S ESCAPE**

**7782**
**THE BATWING: THE JOKER'S**
**AERIAL ASSAULT**

**7783**
**THE BATCAVE: THE PENGUIN**
**AND MR. FREEZE'S INVASION**

**7784**
**THE BATMOBILE: ULTIMATE**
**COLLECTOR'S EDITION**

**7785**
**ARKHAM ASYLUM**

## 2007

**7786**
**THE BATCOPTER: THE**
**CHASE FOR SCARECROW**

**7787**
**THE BAT-TANK: THE**
**RIDDLER AND BANE'S HIDEOUT**

## 2008

**7884**
**BATMAN'S BUGGY: THE**
**ESCAPE OF MR. FREEZE**

**7885**
**ROBIN'S SCUBA JET: ATTACK**
**OF THE PENGUIN**

**7886**
**THE BATCYCLE: HARLEY**
**QUINN'S HAMMER TRUCK**

**7888**
**THE TUMBLER: THE JOKER'S**
**ICE CREAM SURPRISE**

**COMCON016
GREEN LANTERN
MINIFIGURE**

**COMCON017
SUPERMAN
MINIFIGURE**

**COMCON018
BATMAN
MINIFIGURE**

**4526
BATMAN**

**4527
THE JOKER**

**4528
GREEN LANTERN**

**6857
THE DYNAMIC DUO
FUNHOUSE ESCAPE**

**6858
CATWOMAN CATCYCLE
CITY CHASE**

**6860
THE BATCAVE**

**6862
SUPERMAN VS.
POWER ARMOR LEX**

**6863
BATWING BATTLE
OVER GOTHAM CITY**

**6864
BATMOBILE AND THE
TWO-FACE CHASE**

**30160
BAT JETSKI**

**30161
BATMOBILE**

**30164
LEX LUTHOR**

**COMCON020
SHAZAM! MINIFIGURE**

**COMCON022
BIZARRO MINIFIGURE**

**10937**
**BATMAN: ARKHAM**
**ASYLUM BREAKOUT**

**76000**
**ARCTIC BATMAN VS.**
**MR. FREEZE: AQUAMAN ON ICE**

**76001**
**THE BAT VS. BANE:**
**TUMBLER CHASE**

**76002**
**SUPERMAN METROPOLIS**
**SHOWDOWN**

**76003**
**SUPERMAN: BATTLE**
**OF SMALLVILLE**

**76009**
**SUPERMAN: BLACK**
**ZERO ESCAPE**

**5001623**
**JOR-EL**

**COMCON030**
**GREEN ARROW MINIFIGURE**

**COMCON029**
**BLACK SUIT SUPERMAN**
**MINIFIGURE**

**76010**
**BATMAN: THE**
**PENGUIN FACE OFF**

**76011**
**BATMAN: MAN–BAT ATTACK**

**76012**
**BATMAN: THE RIDDLER CHASE**

**76013**
**BATMAN: THE JOKER**
**STEAM ROLLER**

**76023**
**THE TUMBLER**

**5004081**
**PLASTIC MAN**

**COMCON036**
**BATMAN OF ZUR–EN–ARRH**

**COMCON037**
**BATMAN CLASSIC TV SERIES BATMOBILE**

## 2015

**76025**
**GREEN LANTERN**
**VS. SINESTRO**

**76026**
**GORILLA GRODD**
**GOES BANANAS**

**76027**
**BLACK MANTA DEEP**
**SEA STRIKE**

**76028**
**DARKSEID INVASION**

**76034**
**BATBOAT HARBOR PURSUIT**

**76035**
**JOKERLAND**

**76040**
**BRAINIAC ATTACK**

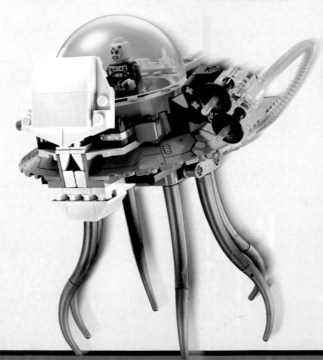

**SDCC2015**
**ACTION COMICS #1 SUPERMAN**

**SDCC2015**
**ARSENAL**

# 2016

**76044**
**CLASH OF THE HEROES**

**76045**
**KRYPTONITE INTERCEPTION**

**76046**
**HEROES OF JUSTICE:**
**SKY HIGH BATTLE**

**76052**
**BATMAN CLASSIC TV**
**SERIES: BATCAVE**

**76053**
**BATMAN: GOTHAM**
**CITY CYCLE CHASE**

**76061**
**MIGHTY MICROS:**
**BATMAN VS. CATWOMAN**

**76062**
**MIGHTY MICROS:**
**ROBIN VS. BANE**

**76063**
**MIGHTY MICROS:**
**THE FLASH  VS. CAPTAIN COLD**

**Project Editor** Emma Grange
**Editor** Tina Jindal
**Senior Designer** Nathan Martin
**Designer** Karan Chaudhary
**Editorial Assistant** Rosie Peet
**Senior Pre-Production**
**Producer** Jennifer Murray
**Managing Editors** Paula Regan,
Simon Hugo, Chitra Subramanyam
**Design Managers** Neha Ahuja, Guy Harvey
**Art Director** Lisa Lanzarini
**Publisher** Julie Ferris
**Publishing Director** Simon Beecroft

**Additional Photography** Markos Chouris,
Christopher Chouris, and Gary Ombler

First American Edition, 2016
Published in the United States by DK Publishing
345 Hudson Street, New York, NY 10014

Page design Copyright © 2016 Dorling Kindersley Limited
DK, a Division of Penguin Random House LLC

17 18 19 20  10 9 8 7 6 5 4
021–283075–Apr/16

DK books are available at special discounts when purchased in
bulk for sales promotions, premiums, fund-raising, or educational
use. For details, contact: DK Publishing Special Markets,
345 Hudson Street, New York, New York 10014
SpecialSales@dk.com

Printed and bound in China

www.LEGO.com
www.dk.com

A WORLD OF IDEAS:
SEE ALL THERE IS TO KNOW

## ACKNOWLEDGMENTS
DK would like to thank Randi Sørensen,
Paul Hansford, Martin Leighton Lindhardt, Maria
Bloksgaard Markussen, Adam Corbally, Daniel
Mckenna, Casper Glahder, Adam Siegmund Grabowski,
John Cuppage, Justin Ramsden, Karl Oskar Jonas
Norlen, Marcos Bessa, Sally Aston, Sven Robin Kahl,
and Mauricio Bedolla at the LEGO Group, Ben Harper,
Thomas Zellers, and Melanie Swartz at Warner Bros.,
Cavan Scott and Simon Hugo for their writing,
and Sam Bartlett for design assistance.